"Children on Layaway"

It's all about

The

Money$$$

By Ron Howard

To Keith & Colleen...
It is a blessing to know you...
God Bless...

RHd

2008

This book is based on a true story; however all the character names and places are fictitious and any resemblance to any organization is entirely coincidental. Some events in this book are products of the author's imagination. This book was written in hopes to bring some awareness to what really goes on in Residential living. This book is based on true stories from Mr. Renaldo, the children and other staff members. These stories come from the years that Mr. Renaldo worked in residential living with children ages six to eighteen. This book is the only place that you will find these stories in writing because most of these companies are very good at hiding the truth. It did not take Mr. Renaldo very long to discover the truth because the company was not trying to hide it. The truth is that it's all about the money and not the welfare of the children or the staff...

I don't expect these companies to change anything because of this book, but hopefully this book will show the kids that someone cares. I want all the kids in Residential living throughout the United States to know that they will always have a voice with me. This is a million-dollar business and the children are getting pennies in services. When will our government step up and do something to help these children? For all the companies who are going to deny that anything in this book is true, my question to you is how in the hell do you sleep at night...

Ron Howard

"Children on Layaway, it's all about the Money$$$"

Ron Howard

Publish By: JACKSON STREET DREAMER PUBLICATIONS

Author Ron Howard
Edited and Published by
Jackson Street Dreamer Publications
ISBN# 978-0-9795119-1-2
LCCN#2008930694
Additional copies of this book are available by mail.
Send $14.99 (Plus $3.75 S&H) made payable to:
Ron Howard
P.O.Box 4322 Pittsburgh, PA 15204
Purchase on web site at
www.jacksonstreetdreamerpublications.com
Amazon.com, Barnes&Noble website, Pittsburgh
Borders Bookstores
Email-jacksonstreetdreamer@yahoo.com

Printed in the U.S.A. by
Morris Publishing
3212 East Highway 30
Kearney, NE 68847
1-800-650-7888

Introduction

almost 40 years ago it was unheard of for a parent to let their child go into Residential Living. Neighborhoods use to all pull together to help a struggling family whether it is food, money or a troubled child. In my neighborhood on a street named "Jackson Street", we didn't have much, but what we had; we shared. We were like one big family on the streets of poverty and crime. If you got caught doing something wrong away from your house; you got beat by every parent on your way back home. When you got home, you would get another beating by your parent. Everyone watched out for each other's children. If you were hungry, the neighbors would feed you if they had it. No one threw old clothes away on Jackson Street; there was always someone who needed them. The whole neighborhood helped raise each child. That was the support system in my neighborhood and it worked. We need more neighborhoods like that today....

If there was a problem, people would ball up their fist and fight it out. These days, everyone wants to pull a gun and shoot it out. The youth have no fear of going to prison or even getting shot. Why is it so easy for the youth to commit "The Ultimate Act of Violence (Murder)?" What kind of violent rage lurks inside the youth of today? Why don't they value life today like they did 40 years ago? Is there something in the air that causing our children to act this way? Is there something in the water they are drinking? Is it the new chemicals that are in everything? Maybe it is just the "Devil". Everyone seems to have an opinion on what is wrong, but who really has an answer that will resolve this problem. Not me. Not the schools. Not the colleges. Not the parents. Not the President. Maybe we should consider going to God for the answers. Asking God for help makes as much sense as anything else that our society has come up with in the past…

I have determined that my life will be dedicated to helping as many troubled youth as I can. I was one of them and I changed my life. I want the youth of today to know that they don't have to play the hand that is dealt to them. I'm hoping that more adults step up and be positive role models. Show these youth that they can make it in this world. The best way to show this is by example, which is the only true form of leadership. There is strength in numbers, so let's all pull together for this cause. We have the numbers so let's use them. To be a mentor, you don't have to be a "Rocket Scientist". You can be a high school graduate with a good job. Some of these youth will drop out of school; they need to know how important it is to have an education; any education is better than none. Most of the black youth in prison don't have High School Diplomas. Our children simply need successful adults to come back to the neighborhoods as positive role models. It doesn't have to be your neighborhood. It can be any neighborhood in any city where you live. The neighborhoods that need you are not hard to find. Just look in any city in the United States. The children are there waiting on you…..

Even if you didn't come from this type of environment (poverty, black), the children still need to meet you. They need to see Black Doctors, Lawyers, Dentists, Preachers, Teachers, Psychologist and so on. You need to make your success personal to them and you can only do that by going into the neighborhoods. The donations that you give at work are appreciated, but that is not all these children need. They probably need to see you more than getting monetary donations; giving money is the easy way. Spend an hour a month (in person) encouraging the children to make positive changes in their lives. I believe there is more value in that. Let's give back a little. A little from everyone adds up to a lot. These children are worth saving, your money and fame does not relieve you of the obligation to help these children in the poor neighborhoods. Step up and be the positive role model that these children so desperately need, I challenge you…..

The story that you are about to read is on "Troubled Youth" and the Institutions who house these children in Residential living. This story is based on true events as witness by Mr. Renaldo's own eyes and ears. He has also listened to real stories from the children and intends to be their voices so that they have a voice in his story. This is only one story, I'm sure there are many more. Most of these stories are covered up by the staff and the supervisors. These are not just stories; these are crimes against troubled youth and these crimes have been going on too long. Most of the time the company says the children are lying about what happened to them. The truth is, most of the time the children are telling the truth. It is easier to cover it up than it is to hire a new employee. This is a high turnover business because these staff do not get paid a lot of money. This is probably why most of the staff working at these institutions isn't qualified to do this kind of work…

He has worked in a Residential setting as a Supervisor/Primary Youth Counselor. He has personally seen what goes on in these places. There will be people who say that all these stories can't be true. These people, who say these stories aren't true; probably have never worked in this field or they are the ones committing the crimes against these children…

These crimes are personal to him because his mother was one of these children in Residential living 65 years ago. She told him stories that would turn your stomach inside out. She didn't have a voice neither when she was in Residential Living, but now she does in his story…

This book was not written for entertainment purposes. It is meant to give the children a voice and to inform the public. More people need to know what really goes on inside the walls of Residential Living. After hearing what goes on with these children, I can honestly say "It is all about the

*money". **God forgive these institutions that make all this money and does hardly anything to help these Troubled Youth. Enjoy the book; the truth is in these pages...***
"*Believe in Change*"

Acknowledgements

First and foremost I would like to thank God because without him none of this can happen. A special thanks to my wife Monica who after 20 years still makes me smile when I see or think of her. You are my friend, lover, wife, college graduate (Pitt 2008) and soul mate; I am blessed to have you here in my life. A special thanks to all the staff that work in Residential living and actually care about the children; you will get your rewards now and later; God bless the staff! A special thanks to Donald Johnson for helping me to get the book ready for print. A special thanks to all my children and nieces. A special thanks to my daughters Lashawna, Sharonna and my niece Danielle for helping me with the typing of my first book. A special thanks to all my family and friends. A special thanks to "Morris Publishing" for doing a great job with the printing of this book. A special thanks to all the staff and faculty at the University of Pittsburgh. A special thanks to my sister "Diane" for supporting me at all my book signings. A special thanks to Joan and Harry Garrett for your support of my first book. A special thanks to all the people who came out to support my book signings. A special thanks to all my new friends on "My Space". A special thanks to all my "Haters" because you have done a great job encouraging me to be better. A special thanks to all the Borders Stores that carry my book and any other stores that was kind enough to give my books a chance...

Chapter 1

"Orientation"

*H*i, my name is Mr. Renaldo and this is my story. This story takes place in a town in Pennsylvania called Hopesville. After getting my hard earned Associate's degree in "Child and Family Studies" in 2004 from the local community college, I started seriously Looking for a job. I only went back to school because I wanted to find more ways of helping these troubled youth. I knew giving them money wasn't the answer because that was only helping them materially. I wanted to learn how to heal their minds and the only way to do that is through education...

My wife Janet and I have been self-employed in the daycare business for over eight years and now it's time to do something else to help these children. We started the daycare business to make money and that slowly changed as I saw these young children from infancy to 13-years old without fathers coming to our daycare. Seeing them reminded me of my troubled past childhood and made me want to do more to help these children. I wanted to find a job working with troubled youth. I just wasn't sure in what capacity. This is something that I knew I could be good at because I had been there where they are and most importantly my heart will be in it. I grew up as a troubled youth and I remember how hard it was for me to make positive changes...

I found a place called "God's Love Institute" on the Internet. Just the name of this place gave me a good warm feeling inside. How can you go wrong with a place that is called God's Love Institute? This organization has been in business for over 100 years and seems to have a great success record. They came highly recommended with a lot of accolades alongside their name...

"Children on Layaway, it's all about the Money$$$"

After only reading about this business for just a few minutes, I knew that this was the place where I wanted to work. I read that the business was founded by some Nuns and the foundation was established with the love of God. The Mission of this institution is to bring family and children back together through love and support. This sounds like my kind of place so I immediately put in my resume. A week later I got a call from God's Love Institute to come in for an interview...

The interview went very well and I got the job. I was excited to get started because I felt like God was leading me down this path. Who would've thought that a man with my background in crime and violence would be working with troubled youth? It would make more sense for me to have been murdered or in prison for my past discretions. God works in mysterious and wonderful ways...

The company told me that I had to go through a week of orientation prior to working with the children. The first day of orientation was very interesting because the first thing we did was pray for 5 minutes with one of the sisters. That felt strange, but refreshing to me. I have never heard of an orientation where a prayer was done before starting. I can't help but feel good about this place now...

There were five other people in the orientation with me. We all looked at each in surprise before bowing our heads to pray. There was one middle aged white lady named Laray. She was medium built with long red hair with pale skin. She was very soft spoken and friendly. There were two other African American males and one fat middle aged white man. There names were Jimmy, Earl and Matt. Jimmy looks like he was in his early twenties, with his hair in dread locks. Earl was probably in his forties and Matt also looked to be in his forties. I felt a little intimidated after the prayer because I was questioning myself as to whether I could live up to the company's seemingly high expectations. After the prayer, the rest of the day was spent on the rules and regulations of the Institute. We started at 9:00am and ended at 5:00pm.

The second day was basically the same, more talk about rules and regulations. We were all having a hard time staying awake. It was really boring; it took everything in my power to keep my eyes open. They gave us so much paper that I had to bring my college book bag to carry all of it home. There was staff in and out of the room all day telling us about different aspects of the job. There must have been at least 5 or 6 different faces from the Institution that came in that day. I couldn't remember all their names. The third day was a little more interesting for us because we met two of the supervisors from "Residential Living" where I expected to work when I was done with orientation. Their names are, Mr. Derek and Mr. Shaw, who are the two main supervisors at the units on campus. They controlled all eight of the boy's units. Their positions are called, "Supervisor of Residential Living". There are "Assistant Supervisors" at every unit who work for Mr. Derek and Mr. Shaw...

I was very curious to hear what the supervisors had to say about working on the units. Mr. Shaw is soft spoken and sounded sincere about everything he said. He is a 35 year old white male, with a bulging built. When Mr. Derek talked, he sounded like a seasoned drug dealer trying to sale some fake drugs to us. He never once looked at us when he talked and he seemed very nervous. He walked around the room as if he had lost something and had no idea where it was at. It was like he was in the street trying to make a drug deal under a street light in downtown Hopesville...

Mr. Derek is about 6feet 3inches tall, weighing about 230 pounds. He is a light skinned African-American with an obvious fake smile on his face. His smile looked like something he had practiced to perfection in a mirror every morning. He has a black suit on looking very professional in spite of what was coming out of his mouth. He reminded me of used car salesman that wasn't very good at what he does, but well enough if you don't know any better. I couldn't honestly get myself to believe a word that came out his mouth. I was hoping that it was my imagination leading me to think that this man is a crook. There is something very evil about this man and what he represents. I know that I would have to watch my back with him because I plan on working in his units...

The fourth day we had CPR and First Aid training. That morning (9:30) at the beginning of class, one of the men was called out of the room and he never returned. We found out later that he didn't pass his drug test. It was Jimmy with the Dread Locks. He looked and acted like a "Weed Head" anyway. He always talked slow and sometimes I thought I smelled marijuana on his clothing. After orientation that day, we were allowed to visit the units on campus. I went to visit St. Johns; this is a unit that housed boys' age five to ten years old. There were eight boys in the dayroom watching television and playing board games. There was two female staff working that day. They were sitting right there with the boys, but not really interacting with them. I introduced myself and went over to where the boys were sitting and playing...

They all gathered around me and begin to ask me questions. One of the kids said, "Hey Mister what unit are you going to be working at? I smiled and said, "I'm not sure yet". He said, "Can you play basketball? I said, yes". One by one each of the kids proudly told me their names and what they'd like to do in the future. I firmly shook each one of the boy's hand and sat down next to the staff. They weren't paying any attention to anything the kids were doing and I felt like they weren't doing their jobs. I observed the boys for about an hour then I went home. While driving I was thinking how nice it is going to be working with the staff and the boys at God's Love Institute...

On the fifth day we learned how to restrain the kids, the way they want us to do it was a joke. The techniques for restraining a kid seemed almost impossible to use, but that is how the company wanted it done. We all went along with it, but we knew that it wasn't going to work in a real situation. Originally I was supposed to work the 3 to 11 shift, but I asked the (Director of Human Resources) named Miss Kate could I work two 16 hour shifts on the weekend and one 8 hour shift during the week. She agreed and now I'm ready to start my career as a "Primary Youth Counselor" at God's Love Institute…

The unit that I'm going to work in is called St. Pauls. All the units on campus are named after Saints. Let's just hope that I'll find some Saints working in the units. This is an all boys Residential Therapeutic Facility (RTF) unit; there are 13 boys living there ranging in age from 13 to 18. The supervisor in charge of this unit is unfortunately Mr. Derek. This is going to be very interesting dealing with his bullshit every week, but it isn't about him. It is always about the kids and making life better for them… **<u>Believe in Change</u>**

Chapter 2

"Meeting the Three Stooges"

My first day of work started on a Friday (3-11) and I was psyched up and ready. This is the path that God has put me on so what could go wrong. The dress code was casual, no uniforms; I wasn't sure what the other staff were going to be wearing on the units. Since I always took enormous pride in my appearance; the dress code was no big deal to me. I always made sure that I was looking good by having the latest fashions in urban wear. I always felt that if the kids see me consistently taking pride in my appearance, than they will do the same. We must lead by example if you want positive results. The children that I am going to work with need strong, positive role models in their troubled lives to make a positive difference. When they see me, I want them to say, "I want to be just like Mr. Renaldo. Kids are constantly watching the adults in their lives so I need to be doing the right things all the time…

I wasn't quite sure what to expect when I went to St. Pauls because I have never worked in this type of environment before. My plan was to just chill and see how the other staff ran things. Hopefully this will help me work with the kids better. Just listening to rumors and gossip from other staff members, my first impression was that all I learned in orientation had nothing to do with how the units are run. I guess I'll find out soon enough how true this is. No matter what the other Staff do on the units, I'm still going to do the right thing for the children. This might piss some of the other staff off, but I don't give a shit. When I go home after work, I'll sleep well because I know I did the right thing…

When I arrived at St. Pauls, the kids were still in school. There is a school on the campus. This is a 5 year old school that educates kids from the units and the children who stay off-campus with their parents. The kids went to school from 7:00am to 3:00pm. Some kids on campus were able to attend Public School, but no kids from St. Pauls qualified for that privilege. There are about 10 classrooms in the building with "Hall Monitors" sitting outside every classroom making sure the kids are doing what they are supposed to do. Hall Monitors are the staff who go in the rooms and violently restrain the kids when they act-out in the classrooms…

There is a minimum of five or six restraints every day at the school. I'm going to be working in a (R.T.F.) unit and almost all of these kids have mental health issues that require them to take many different medications. Sometimes St Pauls will get a kid that is just a delinquent with a "Conduct Disorder" which makes it easier for the staff to work with the kid. Usually these kids just have trouble with discipline. Every child is assigned to this unit for a minimum of 90 days and then they are re-evaluated to see if the child can move to another unit that is less restricted. When a child moves to another unit because of improvement in their behavior, it is called "Stepping Down".

There are probably 100 children on this campus and 95% of them are here through no-fault of their own. It is usually the parents or guardians who have let the child down in some part of their young lives. Most of the time it is "Drug/Alcohol Abuse" and sometimes it is "Sexual Abuse". On rare occasions the parents just can't handle the kids anymore and they need help…

These children have no reason to trust adults because of their negative past experiences with them. Staff or adults have to earn their trust and that is not going to be easy. If the child doesn't trust you, it is almost impossible to help them right away. I believe I can earn the kid's trust through education, consistency, fairness, listening and just being there for the child's basic needs…

"Children on Layaway, it's all about the Money$$$"

The Supervisor/Primary Youth Counselor named Mr. Kojak is sitting in the office when I arrived for my 3 to 11 shift on Friday. He has been working faithfully at God's Love Institute for ten years. He is a white male in his early 30's with a big bald head looking like a "Bouncer" at a nightclub. He is married with no children yet; I don't know how long he has been married. He is about 5' 10", weighing 320 pounds and not much of that is muscle. He has been the Supervisor at St. Pauls for about a year; maybe that is why he lost all of his hair. I'm sure that position has to be very stressful...

Trying to be a supervisor and a counselor at the same time seems almost impossible to accomplish. I can only imagine the problems that he has to contend with on this unit. In my personal and professional opinion, the two positions need to be separate to work properly. That is the only way to get real respect as a supervisor. He introduced himself to me and asked me if I wanted a tour of the unit...

We left the office to look at the day-room, which is a room where the kids play games or just relax. Then we went to the TV-room where there were a few sofas and a 36 inch TV sitting across from the sofa. We traveled down the hall towards the kitchen, which was only about 10 feet away. There were four picnic size tables, about 8 feet long and 2 feet wide sitting in the kitchen area. All the kids could eat at once if necessary, but that wasn't always a good idea because of fights between the kids. The food was delivered to the units pre-cooked so all the staff had to do is heat it up and serve it. There was a large refrigerator sitting in the corner of the kitchen that was full of assorted foods...

We left the kitchen and went upstairs where all the kids' rooms are located. This unit could safely house 14 kids at one time with no problem. We took a look at the children's bedrooms and Mr. Kojak explains how the rooms are supposed to be set up. The rooms were not that big, probably 10 x 15 in size. Some of the rooms had two beds and three of them are singles. There are large bathrooms at both ends of the hall containing two showers and two commodes. The staff has an area to watch television or just relax in the hallway. It looked like a college dormitory to me. Mr. Kojak said, "If there is anything you need than just let him know". I said, "Thanks, everything is fine right now". He smiled and said, "Let's hope it stays that way. I'll talk to you later Mr. Renaldo". I got a good vibe from talking to Mr. Kojak. I felt as though he had a good sincere heart and a kind soul...

When I walked back downstairs I met Mr. Curly, a 50 year old African American male who also had a bald head. He had dark glasses on so I could not see his eyes. I heard a rumor from one of the kids that he only had one eye, but I couldn't tell because of the dark glasses. He has been working at God's Love Institute for 12 years and all the staff seemed to respect him. He started out as a daytime janitor and was promoted 10 years ago to Primary Youth Counselor because of staff shortages on the units. He has been working as a counselor for the past ten years without any educational background in working with troubled youth. The word on campus is that he is legendary for knocking the shit out of kids to get their respect...

His wife is a retired Air Force Sergeant who he speaks very highly of. They have two children, a boy and girl. The boy is in the Military and the girl is still in High school. The first thing he said to me is, "Mr. Renaldo, you are the "No Man" for the next 30 days everything the kids ask you, you tell them no. Even if they ask you to go to the bathroom, you say no". I told him, "No problem, I'll just sit back and see how things work around here". He said, "A lot of these kids are manipulators and they pray off new staff so be careful". It was hard for me to believe that all the rumors about Mr. Curly were true. He seemed like such a nice family man with a good head on his shoulders. I'm going to think positive and hope and pray that the rumors about him abusing kids are not true...

The next Staff I met was Mr. Moe, a 30 year old white male that looks like an "Olympic Power lifter". He only 5' 6" tall, but weighs about 340 pounds. He wears his hair in a pony tail like a "Japanese Sumo Wrestler". I would bet money that he is on steroids because I don't believe you can naturally get that kind of muscle without it. He is not married but lives with the mother of his two young kids. He told me, "The best way to control the kids on the unit is by putting a lot of physical pain on them when they first arrive. The story about him on campus is that he is a constant (Complainer); he bitches about everything. People hate talking to him because he cries the blues all the time. No one wants to hear a grown man crying all the time, especially one that weighs 340 pounds. He works a lot of overtime to pay his bills like many of the other staff on campus. That is probably why he is bitching all the time…

I met Mr. Stan a little later upstairs sitting in the hallway writing in his little black notebook. He is an African American male, in his late thirties who looks like a professional football player. Mr. Stan and Mr. Moe are best friends and grew up the same little town. Mr. Stan has been working for God's Love Institute for ten years as a Hall Monitor during the school year. He is not married, but has a son with his high school sweetheart. He has a real deep voice; you can hear him whispering 30 feet away. Mr. Stan is known around campus as a playboy and an avid weight lifter like Mr. Moe. He also works a lot of overtime, up to a hundred hours a week. The other staff says that he will fall asleep right in the middle of a conversation because he is so tired all the time…

I introduced myself to him and he said in a deep echoing voice, "It's about time this company hired someone new, we need some help around here". I smiled and said, "I'm here to help, let me know if you need me to do something". He smiled and said, "We are cool right now, lets hope that it stays this way. We got some crazy ass kids up in here now, so watch out". I told Mr. Stan thanks and shook his hand. The 3 to 11 shift was real quiet that day. I went home at 11:00pm to get ready for my daylight shift at 7 a.m. By the time I got to sleep that night it was

1 a.m. and I had to wake up at 5:30 a.m. to get ready to come back to work. It's going to be rough working like this, but we all have to make sacrifices in life…

That next morning I met Mr. Larry and Mr. Jackson, they are the weekend staff. Mr. Larry is a white male in his early 30's, with a short military hair cut. He has been working for God's Love Institute for three years. I heard that he has been moved to several different units because of his heavy handed tactics on the kids. He is a body builder, with apparently more muscle than brain. St. Pauls is supposed to be his last stop for working with kids because of all the Child-Lines he has got in the past. He is another staff who believes that the more he beats a kid up, the less likely the child is going to mess with the staff again. He is married with two young kids…

He proudly tells everyone that he use to be in the "Marines". He sports a Marine tattoo on his arm to show his pride in being an ex-marine. The rumor on campus is that he never made it out of "Boot Camp". All the staff that I have talked to said don't trust him because he is a snake and a snitch. When I introduced myself to Mr. Larry that morning, he never stopped talking. He must have talked for two straight hours nonstop about everything he could think of. I was sorry that I introduced myself to him. I felt like choking him after 15 minutes of listening to him moan and groan about this company. I hope he's not like that every morning because I don't know if I could stand it. I like peace and quiet in the morning and if I do have to listen to someone, it certainly wouldn't be anyone like Mr. Larry. I don't know what kind of coffee he had before he got here, but it must be real strong. I had visions of knocking him out just to shut him up. I decided to be nice and act like I was listening to him, but after a few minutes his words were just noise filling the air. I can't remember one word he said the whole two hours he was talking…

In between Mr. Larry running his mouth, which was only short periods of time; I and Mr. Jackson got to say a few words to each other. He is a white male in his early 30's. He is about six feet tall, loves to play basketball and run the track that is located on the campus. He is very active, he believes in keeping the kids physically busy and I like that. He is quiet compared to big mouth Mr. Larry. Thank God for that! Mr. Jackson only weakness is that he appears to be a follower and he is following the other dumb ass staff on the unit right now. His wife also works at God's Love Institute as a Therapist and he also has a sister who works here in education as a teacher. His sister is the one who got him his job. He has been working here for three years and seems content with being a primary youth counselor. He has no college education so I don't know what else he could do out in the real world. Mr. Jackson is one of the rare few who do not work any overtime to supplement his income. Maybe that's because his wife makes decent money as a therapist...

When Sunday evening came I was dead tired because I was not used to working that many hours in a row. The two 16 hour shifts were beginning to get to me; I can feel it in my body and mind. I know that it's going to take me some time to get use to working these long weekends. I wouldn't want to work like this for a long period of time; maybe a year at the most. I just need to do this until I get my degree from the University of Hopesville. The good news is that it was a quiet weekend and I don't have to come back here until Friday afternoon at 3 pm...

I will spend more time next week getting to know the kids a little better. In orientation, they advised us to read the files on the kid's background so that we knew their problems before we meet them. I would rather get to know the kid first and read their files later because sometimes kids change after the files are written. The files are not always accurate; they just basically give you a background on the child's problems. I didn't want to poison my mind with the child's past history. The staff told me a little about each kid, but I want to see how they act around me. It's possible that the child could be the complete opposite in my presence. This is what I want and I need to find out for myself...

When Sunday evening came (around 6:00pm); I was really tired. Hopefully, I will get used to working like this. I really don't have a choice because I go to college full time during the week. I already have a degree in "Child and Family Studies", now I am going for a degree in "Child Psychology". My wife Janet is also going to college studying the same thing. We are doing all this and still running a daycare at our house. We are very busy people with very little time for relaxation. We also have two daughters Moonie and Sunshine ages 20 and 15, who take up a lot of our time. Janet and I are blessed to have two typical daughters in this day and age. There are so many kids in this society doing the wrong thing that you have to consider yourself blessed to have children that are doing what they are supposed to do. I just can't thank God enough for Moonie and Sunshine...

My first 40 hours on the unit was quiet and I hope that it stays that way. None of the kids acted out and the staff were on their best behavior. I didn't really get to personally meet any of the kids. I'll spend more time getting to know them next week. I expect to get along fine with the kids; it's the staff that I think that I'm going to have problems with. I don't agree with the way they approach dealing with the kids physically and mentally. Hopefully I can change their thinking and things will get better on the units. Slapping the kids upside their heads is not the answer. None of the staff have any education in working with troubled youth. This is going to be a problem because I'm not a teacher and some of the staff is too old to try to teach something new... *"Believe in Change"*

Chapter 3

"Meeting the Kids"

$\mathcal{T}$he first kid I met was Isaiah; he is big 16 years old, He is about 5'8" with black curly hair, weighing about 250. He is an African American teenager who is here because he got in trouble at school. His mother or father is not involved in his life and his grandmother has been raising him since he was a baby. The grandmother sent him to God's Love Institute because she could no longer handle him. He told me that he used to weight 300 pounds a year ago and just recently started to lose weigh. He said that he has been working out by playing basketball and lifting weights…

He started bragging to me about how he was restrained for 16 hours at his last placement. I told him that a restraint shouldn't have taken that long, someone must have been doing something wrong. It should never take that long to calm a kid down. He smiled and said, "Well every time they let me up I tried to punch one of the staff and they would start the restraint all over again". I told him, "Well you don't have to worry about me restraining anyone that long. I don't believe in restrains unless the kid is trying to hurt me, himself or another kid". He smiled saying, "We'll see", as I walked out of his room. Isaiah's room was right across from where the staff sat so they could keep an eye on him. He was a kid who needed to be observed at all times; he is very intelligent and sneaky. This is not a good combination for the staff to deal with…

Then I met Daniel, a little skinny white kid who always had a smile on his face. The other staff told me to watch out for him because he has a history of biting and scratching staff during

24

restraints. He has long dirty fingernails and big teeth, he reminded me of an "albino rat". Daniel told me that he likes picking through garbage and taking things apart to see how they work. He said, "Mr. Renaldo my dream is to be garbage man someday. My adopted family always rides around looking for other people's trash". Then he says, "One man's trash is another man's gold". I told him, "If that is what makes you happy, then you should go for your dreams"…

I heard from another staff that Daniel and his younger brother were sexually abused as young children. They were locked in the basement of their house for months before anyone found out about it. They were only toddlers when they were abused. I can only imagine the mental scars that these kids have on their minds. They have been in placement all their lives and are mentally institutionalized. Daniel is 16 years old and his brother is 15. His brother is in another placement across town. I think Daniel and I are going to get along fine as long as he doesn't bite me…

I ran into Jonah later on that day; he is a 15 year old African American kid. He is short, about five feet tall and stocky. He likes to lift weights and play basketball every chance he gets. He has four other siblings who are in placement; he is the oldest and probably the meanest of all his brothers and sisters. Jonah is here because his mother is a drug addict and father is no where to be found. This has made him a very bitter young man, so he is very rebellious at times. He doesn't mind challenging staff mentally and physically. He is used to physical confrontations from the staff, but I am going to be different. I expect to talk my way through any problems with him. I explained to him that I don't believe in restraints unless I have to. He said, "I never heard staff say that before". I said, "Well your hearing it now". He smiled and said, "That's good", than he laid across his bed with a smile on his face…

Meeting Joel was unusual because his father is a "State Senator". Joel has sexual issues that his parents could not afford for the public to find out about. He has homosexual tendencies and has been known to come back from a home-visit with his 7 year old sister's panties hidden in his clothes. Just by talking to him, you couldn't tell that he has these problems. He was very polite and seems like a typical adolescent. He loves to skateboard outside and loves attempting some very challenging moves. He likes to brag to the other kids about how much money his parents have. He is a thin, 16 year old white male, about 5'8". He said, "Mister, I heard that you don't restrain people. Why don't you restrain?" I said, "Most restrains are unnecessary so I only do them if I have to". With a sound of attitude in his voice he said, "Yeah, they are unnecessary", and walked away...

Just through my observation, I knew that this kid named Ezekiel was going to be a problem. He always seemed to have a chip on his shoulder. No matter what the staff asked him to do, he always had something smart to say. I sat down on the bench outside near the field where he was sitting and introduced myself to him. I said, "Hi, my name is Mr. Renaldo, what's your name?" He said, "Its Ezekiel, and I hope that you're not going to be an asshole like these other staff here". I firmly said, "First thing you need to do is watch your language when I'm around you and we won't have any problems". He got up and defiantly said, "Yeah, your going to be just like the other ones", and then he walked away. Ezekiel is 16 years old and is basically a delinquent whose father couldn't handle anymore. He is a white kid, about 6'2" with dusty brown hair. The first thing I noticed when I sat next to him was his long dirty fingernails. He looked like a throwback to the old "Hippie Days" of the 60's. I knew from our first meeting that he was going to be a problem. There was attitude written all over his face...

I was warned about meeting a kid named Hosea; staff told me that every word that comes out of his mouth is a lie. Staff calls him "Hosea the Molester", because in his records it reads that he molested his younger brother. He is 17 years old and his younger brother is 12 years old. Hosea molested his brother when he was eight years old at their home. That is how he got put in placement and this is where it's going to stay until he is 18 years old and signs himself out. He is a white kid with a short stocky build. I shook his hand and introduced myself to him. He smiled and said, "Mister, I'm getting out of here this summer, boy I can't wait". I said, "Congratulations, what are you going to do once you get out?" He said, "I'm going to Community College". I told him "That's a great idea; I started there myself". I was happy to hear one of these kids actually mention college, even if he is just lying about going, at least he talking about it...

The kids that I met so far were surprised that I was willing to shake their hands. The other staff won't shake hands with the kids because they are scared of getting germs from them. That's got to be some of the dumbest shit that I've heard in my life. What kind of germs does the staff think they can get from these kids? As long as you're washing your hands on regular basis, germs will be one of the last things the staff has to worry about working on the units. I think that is being disrespectful not to at least have the courtesy to shake a kid's hand...

In my opinion these kids are treated more like inmates than troubled youth. This is not a prison; the kids should be treated accordingly. This has a lot to do with the educational level and the mentality of most of the staff on campus. Most of the staff that works here shouldn't be working with kids anyway; they should be working with prisoners. I can see that there is a long road ahead of me if I expect to make a positive difference in these young children's lives...

A (R.T.F Unit) is supposed to have one staff to every 3.5 kids. Every unit on campus is short-staffed, so there is a lot of staff who work overtime. The other staff told me that it has been like this for a long time. It is hard for this company to hire the most qualified people because they refuse to pay appropriate salaries for people with the degrees. So far everything at my unit has been very quiet. Maybe it is "The quiet before the storm", time will always tell. Next week I get to meet the rest of the kids.

"Children on Layaway, it's all about the Money$$$"

That should be interesting for me and for them. I've heard that some of the other staff at the other units is an extraordinary bunch of characters also. I can't wait to meet them...
"Believe in Change"

Chapter 4

"Stress can kill"

Several months later on a Saturday morning (9:30), I observed Isaiah suspiciously passing a small black suitcase across the hall. I calmly asked him what was in it; he said nervously, "Nothing mister, I borrowed it last week and I'm just returning it". I told him that the suitcase sure looked like it had something in it by the way you were carrying it. A few seconds later I decided to go in the other boy's room (Hosea) and see what was in the suitcase. It was still sitting on the floor near the door because Hosea hadn't picked it up yet. I quickly grabbed it and carried the suitcase to the hallway so Isaiah could see what I was doing. The suitcase felt like there was something in it because it was too heavy to be empty...

Isaiah slowly came to his door and said, "Mister, why are you opening up that suitcase?" I looked at him and said, "Don't worry everything is going to be okay". He said, "There are only some underclothes in the bag so why don't you believe me?" In a low voice I said, "I believe you, but it's my job to look in this suitcase". When I went through the suitcase I found a four pound bag of assorted candy hidden behind some old t-shirts. I firmly told Isaiah, "You know that you are not permitted to have candy in your rooms". He angrily said, "That's not mine, I don't know how that damn candy got into that suitcase". I said in a calm voice, "Don't worry everything is going to be okay". He walked back into his room mumbling and saying "What the fuck do you mean its going to be okay?" I said in an even calmer voice, "It's going to be okay". I could tell that he didn't expect me to be this understanding about the situation. He is not used to staff behaving in this manner The way that I was handling this must be new to him...

Five minutes later Isaiah came to his doorway and shouted angrily, "That's my fucking shit and I want it right now". He started walking towards me slowly and cautiously. Not knowing what to expect, I put the suitcase down and faced him slowly as he got closer. When I did that, he stopped and loudly said, "Give me my shit right now". He was about four feet away from me now. I was mentally and physically preparing myself for my first restraint, but surprisingly he didn't move any closer. I told him once again as I still tried to remain calm, "It's going to be okay, just relax". I made sure that I kept calmness in my voice because I know how important voice regulation is when you're trying to de-escalate a situation. I knew that he was used to situations similar to this ending in a physical restraint...

Unfortunately I was the only staff upstairs at the time so I have to be careful how I handle this situation. I don't know if the other staff could hear what was going on. I told Isaiah, "Look this is no big deal, don't try to make it more than what is really is. I'm going to hold on to the candy and you can get it back when you go back home next week". He has a seriously confused look on his face after I said that. He went back into his room and then laid across his bed. A few minutes later I went to the door of his room and said, "We can talk more about this later and thank you for letting me do my job". He didn't say anything as I walked back to the staff's chairs and sat down. I was happy that I was able to de-escalate that situation without physical violence. I firmly believe that most restraints are just a matter of a staff's ego being hurt. These are things you learn with the proper education and training. Hopefully the way I handled this situation will encourage other staff to try to follow my example. The best way to lead is by example...

When I told the other staff what happened, they were surprised that I didn't have to restrain Isaiah. They know that Isaiah has an extensive history of being restrained for almost anything. I told Mr. Larry and Mr. Jackson that I stayed calmed and eventually my calmness settled him down. I also made sure that I didn't get into his personal space which I believe is about 3 feet out from the center of the body. A lot of times staff members make the mistake of getting in a kids space and a physical restraint will occur. You really don't need to get in their space if they are not hurting themselves or someone else. Mr. Larry said, "We should keep that candy for ourselves, fuck him". I told him, "No, I promised Isaiah that I would let him take the candy back home and I'm a man of my word". Mr. Larry angrily said, "Well I wouldn't have promised that asshole shit. He shouldn't have brought the candy to the unit". I told him again that I'm a man of my word and I'm going to be known for that by the kids and staff. Mr. Jackson smiled and said, "If that's what it takes to keep Isaiah quiet, then I'm all for it. No one wants to restrain that big motherfucker anyway". I think Mr. Jackson appreciated the way I handled the situation, but it's going to take some time before that dumb ass Mr. Larry understands...

An hour later when all the kids were downstairs, I called Isaiah into the office. He said in an agitated voice, "What did I do now Mister?" I calmly said, "Nothing, I just wanted to tell you what was going to happen for bringing candy on the unit". I told him to sit down and relax. He sat down hesitantly because the other staff doesn't let the kids sit down in the office. The staff are worried about catching some kind of germs from the kids. This is crazy for the staff to be thinking like that, maybe they are crazy. I know they are ignorant and mean to the kids most of the time. I told Isaiah that he can have his candy back next week, but if I catch him with any more candy then I'm going to keep it. I told him that I was just going to take some points off his daily log for what happened today. He smiled and said, "Thank you mister, I thought you were going to give me level one (lowest level in the unit) for a week".

I said, "Isaiah why would I punish you for a whole week because you had one violation of the rules?" He said, "That's what the other staff does so I figured that you would be the same way". I told him that he can expect me to be fair and reasonable all the time, not just today. I think I'm being fair with you and that's who I am. He smiled and shook my hand as he said thank you again. I know he is not used to the staff treating him fairly and he probably thinks that I will change in time. However Isaiah and the other kids will find out that I won't change. I hope that he doesn't take the way I treated him as a sign of weakness. I know that he is from the streets and most street wise kids pray on the weaknesses of others. He would be making a humongous mistake, because I am from the streets also. I'm an educated street person and not too much can get pass me if I don't want it to...

I have heard about restraints in St. Pauls, but there hasn't been any while I was at work. Maybe this is because the other staff doesn't trust me. If I see one of their illegal restraints I'm going to definitely tell management. I hope the unit stays like that because it would really bother me to see the staff abuse their authority over the children in front of me. I want to be a team player, but if that means abusing the kids then I don't want to be on that team. Some of the kids told me about kids getting restrained while I wasn't at work, but nothing was ever put in writing about the restraints. The kids would mention a restraint briefly, but never really went into detail about how and where it happened. I have never told the staff that I don't believe in restraints, but I'm sure the kids did...

I'm sure the other staff are going to show their true colors as soon as they get more comfortable with working with me. So far, the first few months at this unit have been mostly quiet compared to the stories I heard from the other staff on campus when I first started working here. Maybe my presence has made a positive difference in how the staff are going to treat the kids. If that is the case, then my job is going to be so much easier. However, this just might be the (Quiet before the Storm).

One day at the smoking area I met a nice young lady named Sally. She is a white 28-year-old mother of a five year old boy who she is very proud of. She began to tell me about all the problems she is having working at one of the girl's unit. She told me that she has only been working here for a few weeks as the Weekend staff, doing two 16 hour shifts and eight hours on a weekday. All the time she was talking, she is constantly complaining about having a consistent headache that that get worse every time she went to work. She told me that she got the headache the first day she started working on the units; I laughed and said "Join the club"!

Miss Sally told me that all the staff on the unit wouldn't talk to her so she couldn't get any help with the children when she needed it. When she comes in the unit, all the staff give her the silent treatment from 7 a.m. to 11 p.m. and she is not sure why. She said that when she would come to the unit and sit down, all the other staff (which is all African-American females) would leave the floor and she would be there alone with all the children. Sometimes they would leave her alone for hours and this would cause a lot of confusion for the children. Miss Sally had no idea how to run a unit and this made life very difficult and stressful for her…

My advice to her is to ask Mr. Derek to move her to another unit where that she would hopefully be welcomed. She agreed with me and said that she would ask him next week when she saw him. I hope that she does get out that unit because she is really looking stressed out and that is not how a job is supposed to make you feel…

I saw her that following week and she told me that Mr. Derek could not move her right now. She was really upset to the point that tears begin to appear in her eyes. I told her that if Mr. Derek could not give her what she wanted, than she was allowed to go above his head and talk to his supervisor. She seemed very concerned about going above Mr. Derek's head so she said that she would just try to stick it out for little longer. I tried to give her some confidence by saying that things will get better and God only gives you what you can handle in life. I don't know how effective I was because she was still looking seriously stressed when she left…

A few months had passed before I seen Miss Sally again because she had quit smoking cigarettes. I noticed that she was pregnant now; she told me that she was eight months pregnant and looking forward to having her second child. I told her congratulations and wished her the best of luck. I was surprised and concerned that Mr. Derek had her still working on the units and she was so far along in her pregnancy. To me this showed no consideration for her motherly condition...

These children on the units can be very violent at times and can cause physical and emotional pain to the staff. It would be very easy for her to lose her baby if she had to do a violent restraint. I hope for her sake that she gets off these units very soon because it is simply too unsafe for pregnant mother to be working among violent children. Sometimes I just don't know what the supervisors and this company are thinking about...

A week later while I was down at the smoke area I heard that Miss Sally had died on the unit. On a Sunday morning when Miss Sally got to the unit, the other staff left her alone with the kids as they usually do and when the staff came back they found her quietly sitting in a chair in a hallway as if she was asleep. All the kids were still in the bed sleeping so they didn't even notice her sitting there. When the staff saw Miss Sally, they figured that she was just asleep so they didn't even try to wake her up until an hour later when it was time for lunch. When they couldn't wake her up that is when they called 911 and paramedics came to the unit...

Paramedics worked frantically on Miss Sally, but they couldn't do anything to bring her back to consciousness. She was given oxygen and carried out on a stretcher in front of all the kids. They rushed her to the hospital and put her on life support because she quit breathing on her own while on the way. This was an attempt to save her baby because it didn't look good for her...

The doctors discovered that Miss Sally had an aneurysm while she was at work. The doctors said that the stress of the job

34

probably brought the aneurysm on even more rapidly and she should have never been put in a position like that. This is why she was constantly having excruciating headaches on the job. The doctors say that if they could have got to her sooner they would have been able to save her life...

She was on life-support for a few more weeks and then they delivered the baby. She had a healthy baby girl that would have made her very proud if she would have been alive to see her. I really believe this young lady would have been alive if the company would have been more attentive to what was going on with her on the units. All that stress that the other staff was putting on her had to have something to do with her dying so suddenly at such a young age...

A week after the baby was born, the family had a funeral for Miss Sally and some of the children from the unit came. The children really felt badly for Miss Sally and they thought that going to her funeral would be the least that they could do considering how bad the staff treated her. The children pestered the staff so much that they finally gave in and decided to take a few of the girls to the funeral...

The only thing the company did was send a big bouquet of flowers to the funeral, but no one from management came to give their condolences to Miss Sally's family. My family and I went to the funeral and it was very sad. One of the family members was holding the newly born child that will never get to know his mother. I wish I had been able to do more for Miss Sally; I wish the company would have been able to do more. Now she is with God and I'm sure everything is going to be okay. I am not sure if this company is ever going to be okay if this is what I can expect from them... **"Believe in Change"**

Chapter 5

"Mr. Curly sends a Message"

*W*hile sitting in the TV room with a few kids, I hear Mr. Curly shouting angrily at one of the kids in the kitchen. It was on a Friday, around 6:00pm (dinner time). Mr. Curly was telling this kid named Amos that he had to eat all his food or he couldn't get any desert. Amos is new in this unit; he has only been here for a few weeks. He is a 16 year old white male, average height and weight; he is here because he is a delinquent. Amos told Mr. Curly that he couldn't eat all that nasty food and most of the time the food is difficult to eat. He told Mr. Curly that he had no right denying him desert. Mr. Curly told Amos to clear his plate and get out of his kitchen. When a kid clears his plate, he gets up and empties it in the trash and then takes the plate to the kitchen sink to rinse it off. After listening to the conversation for a few more minutes, I told the kids that were watching TV with me to stay right there. I went in the kitchen to see what was going on because I never heard Mr. Curly talking like that before to a kid…

I got in the kitchen just as Mr. Curly pushed Amos in the back as he was walking out of the kitchen. He pushed him so hard that Amos banged his head firmly on the kitchen door. Amos quickly turned around grabbing his head in pain saying, "Keep your fucking hands off me, you one eyed motherfucker". He slowly turned away from Mr. Curly and started walking out of the kitchen again. Just as he got in the doorway, Mr. Curly quickly grabbed him from behind and viciously choked him down to the floor. All the kids were shocked to see Mr. Curly attack Amos the way he did; I know I was incredibly surprised. It looked like a scene that you might see in a neighborhood bar after several hours of drinking hard liquor…

Amos was trying to get him off, but Mr. Curly had a choke hold on his neck which caused Amos to desperately struggle to breathe. In reality, this whole scenario only took about 30 seconds, but in my mind everything was moving in big screen slow motion...

They both went crashing down to the floor in one loud thump with Mr. Curly landing on Amos's back. Mr. Curly's thick black glasses went flying across the floor, landing near my feet. I quickly reached down and picked them up for him. I put the glasses on top of the refrigerator so no other damage would come to them. I asked Mr. Curly did he need me to do anything because I wasn't sure what to do in this situation. He said, "Just grab his legs and straighten them out for me". I did and then he got on top of Amos's back in a more secure position. Amos is still trying to resist, but Mr. Curly has too much weight on top of him now. Mr. Curly looks back at me and says in between deep breaths, "I got this now; you just keep an eye on the other kids". The other kids (five of them) were just sitting there eating their food as if nothing was going on. None of the kids tried to get out the seats to see what was happening to Amos. I guess they are accustomed to seeing this type of behavior, but this is all new to me...

This was the first time I saw a restraint and the first time I saw Mr. Curly without his glasses on. The story on campus must be true about him having one eye because his left eye doesn't fucking move when he looks at me. He really looks like a crazy man on top of this poor kid. I'm going to have to remember to thank him for keeping his glasses on because he sure is an ugly motherfucker without them. I will never get used to doing restraints and I'll never get used to seeing Mr. Curly's one eye staring at me. It just sits there in the eye socket like its dead or not real...

The kids started asking me for more food while I was standing there watching Mr. Curly restrain Amos. It is scary how these kids can block this restraint out of their minds so easily and still be concerned about eating. It is like they are afraid to show emotion; the kids should be emotional about another kid being restrained. I told them that they needed to wait until the restraint was over to get more food. Five minutes later, I'm thinking that it should be over very soon because poor Amos is no longer resisting. Now I was hearing Amos moaning loudly in pain out in the hallway. I quickly walked over to the door to see what's going on because his sounded liked the kid is slowly dying. I was beginning to get sick to my stomach when I saw what Mr. Curly was doing to Amos...

Mr. Curly is taking the point of his elbow and pushing it deep into the middle of Amos's fragile back. My first thought is to break this shit up right now, but I have to keep an eye on the other five kids. Five minutes later, the kids are really starting to get restless because they are still patiently waiting on some more food. I'm not sure if their restlessness is because they were still hungry or because Mr. Curly was taken so long. I can hear the kids whispering to each other as they twist and turn in their chairs. Most of the kids were laughing quietly, which I thought was a little unusual since one of their peers is out in the hallway getting abused...

Amos is moaning much louder now as sweat rolls off his head onto the floor creating a slipping hazard. I'm sure someone could probably hear Amos outside if they were walking pass the unit. He sounds like a wild desperate animal trapped in a bear trap in the woods. I have never heard such painful pleads for mercy coming from a human being before. This went on for ten additional minutes and I just couldn't mentally take it anymore. I reached down and tapped Mr. Curly on his shoulder and quietly said that's enough. He looked at me with that one eye and said in a deep satanic voice, "Let me make sure this kid understands where I'm coming from". He purposely dug his elbow in Amos's back one last time and he begged even louder for mercy...

I wanted to mess Mr. Curly up the same way he abused that poor kid. It took everything in my power to control the urge to kick him in the head. When Mr. Curly finally and reluctantly got off Amos, he just laid there crying loudly. He wasn't moving at all, I thought the poor kid was possibly paralyzed from the neck down. I felt very uncomfortable because I felt like I should have done something to help Amos. I had no contingency plan for something like this, but next time this happens I will. It is hard to plan for something like this because you never know how you're going to react. Mr. Curly walked back into the kitchen and continued feeding the kids again like nothing happened. He acted like there wasn't a kid in the hallway crying because he illegally restrained him…

Ten minutes later, after all the kids were done eating he lined all the kids up in the hallway where Amos still laid sobbing with his face buried into his arms. After two minutes of the kids staring at Amos lying defeated mentally and physically on the floor, Mr. Curly proudly said let's go upstairs. He told the kids that it was time to start their showers and phone calls for the evening. One by one, the kids slowly stepped over Amos as he laid a broken kid on the dirty floor of the hallway. I stayed with Amos to make sure he was going to be okay. I was hoping that there wasn't anything physically wrong with him, other than having some scrapes and bruises. Since I study Psychology, I knew that he would have mental scars for years to come because what Mr. Curly did today; maybe I will also…

I carefully helped Amos up off the floor and walked him outside to get some fresh air. He wasn't very steady on his feet so I wisely supported him the first few minutes. I didn't say anything to him for about five minutes. Then I told Amos that if he felt that he wasn't restrained properly then he should report it. He said "Mr. Curly has been doing this for years from what I heard from the other kids so what difference will it make if I report this restraint. Nothing is going to happen to him because no one at this company gives a shit". I told him in empathetic voice, "Well that doesn't make it right and if it is not right then you should report it". Amos angrily said, "If someone cared, then he wouldn't still be working here". I said with a firm voice,

"I care and I will back you up if you want to file a complaint. I can't help you unless you file a written complaint". He said quietly, "I have to think about it because I don't want any more shit from the other staff at the unit for being a snitch"...

After about 15 minutes of slowly walking around the track on the field, I escorted him back inside the unit. When we got upstairs, Mr. Curly was sitting in the staff's area in the hallway letting one of the kids make a phone call home. Amos purposely put his head down and hurried pass Mr. Curly without looking at him. Amos was like a rabbit sneaking pass a big grizzly bear in fear of being eaten for dinner. I reluctantly sat down next to Mr. Curly, but didn't say anything to him. I just wasn't sure what to say to this idiot. I wanted to find out what goes on in a mind like his; a mind that can hurt children and seemingly not give a damn. The walk outside helped me as much as it helped Amos because I don't know what I would have said if I would have talked to Mr. Curly right after the restraint happened. Five minutes later, the kid who was on the phone finished his phone call and went back to his room creating an opportunity for me and Mr. Curly to talk...

Mr. Curly turned to me with a devilish smile on his face and confidently said, "Do you know why I did that boy like that?" My first thought to that question was that he is a retarded bastard and possessed by the devil. However what came out my mouth was, "No I'm not sure, maybe you can explain it to me so I can understand". He smiled and said, "I wanted to send a message to the other kids so that they know I'm not to be messed with. I wanted them to hear the agonizing pain that Amos was feeling". I calmly said, "Do you think that is the way to do it?" He said, "I have been doing this for a long time and this is the best way to get through to these kids. It is the only thing that the kids understand". Thinking to myself: "This fool is crazier than I thought. I have to get him away from these kids before he kills someone". Mr. Curly said, "You just have to make sure that there are no marks on the kid, just in case of a Child-Line.

I know how to mess the kid up without leaving any marks on their body. I'm a professional, he said proudly. Amos will definitely think twice before he messes with me again"…

A Child-Line is when a kid reports an abuse by a staff member in writing or verbally to the staff's supervisor. In St. Pauls, the report would go to Mr. Derek. Mr. Curly is familiar with getting Child-Lined; he says that it's no big deal. Once a report is made, the staff gets moved to another unit until the investigation is done. This usually takes about three days and if the supervisor finds no grounds to the allegation, he sends the staff back to his unit. Most of the time, the complaint never goes further than Mr. Derek from what I hear from the other staff. Most of the Child-Lines are covered up by him because he does not want to do all the additional paperwork…

From what I understand this has been going on for years. Even if the Department of Welfare (D.P.W.) gets involved, I hear that is also just a joke. Everyone seems to go through the motions, but nothing ever happens to the staff. No wonder these kids don't complain anymore about being abused; it's futile…

When the staff comes back to the unit, unfortunately he/she are usually not very happy that the child filed a complaint against them. From what I hear, there will be some retaliation against the kid by all the staff on the unit. The staff uses this type of harassment to deter any future complaints from the children. This becomes a very volatile situation for the kid because he/she never knows when the staff is going to get their revenge. I'm sure that this is the reason a lot of kids don't do a Child-Line in most situations. I will do my best to watch out for Amos, but I'm not here everyday so I can only do but so much. I'm only one person; he is going to need more than just me to watch out for him. I know that God will continue to keep an eye out for these children also…

The kids that have been in placement for awhile understand how the system works. From a psychological point of view, the emotional scarring has to be more harmful than the physical abuse or equally as bad. After a couple of years of being abused mentally and physically by staff, what are the chances of these children being a positive asset to our society? Does anyone else give a damn other than my wife and me? Is this a battle that I can win without the help of other strong, educated men and women? I know with the help of God and more education, I will have a chance. I doubt if Amos files a complaint against Mr. Curly because he realizes the consequences for writing a complaint. He didn't sound like he was; maybe the fear of retaliation is just too much for him... *"Believe in Change"*

Chapter 6

"A family affair"

$\mathcal{A}$ few weeks later, I still wasn't sure what to do about the restraint that Mr. Curly did to Amos. I was waiting for Amos to file a complaint, but he decided that it wouldn't be in his best interest to do so. Considering the way the Child-Line system works, he is probably right. That's pretty sad for that to be a reality of living in residential. I thought about filing a complaint, but if it didn't go anywhere then I would be stuck with working in a hostile environment, plus I still haven't met anyone yet who I thought could do something to these abusers. If I start making waves now, it would be too easy for a company to fire me. So I decided to write down the events that I witness or the stories that I hear from the kids and other staff. I'll just wait for the appropriate time to tell the proper authorities and I'll have some documentation to back it up. I have to find out who I can trust before I say anything. I'll just continue to write in my notebook; maybe I'll write a book someday about this bullshit if I put enough information together. For now I'll continue to pray and educate myself on how this business works...

My lovely wife Janet decided that she wanted to work with troubled youth in spite of all the stories that I've been telling her. This company certainly could use another caring and loving soul. At least she knows what to expect from this place after the stories I told her. That would be good because she won't come in with high expectations like I did. She accepted a position as a Primary Youth Counselor. She told me that she would be working at the girl's unit (St. Micahs). The girls there are ages 12 to 18 and very unpredictable and act out more than the boys units. From what I hear from the other staff, the girls are more emotional than the boys. Luckily, Janet's unit is on the same campus as St. Pauls. It is only a few units away and she will be working the same shift as me. I'm very happy about that because we are very close and now will be able to see each other more. I was starting to miss her on the weekends and my marriage is very important to me...

Our only concern with both of us working on the weekend together is our 15 year old daughter Sunshine. Her having the whole house to herself and being a typical teenager could potentially be a problem for us. We trusted her, but the fact is that teenagers don't always do what they are supposed to do. Janet and I explained the house rules to Sunshine in real simple words. They were real basic, they went something like this, "No boys, No boys and No damn boys in this house or we are going to kill you"...

The good thing about where Janet worked was that I could walk to her unit in a few minutes if I wanted to see her. So every time we took a break, we would make arrangements over the phone to see each other. We were planning on doing this several times a shift because we got emotional energy from each other. We needed any edge we could get especially with the kids and staff that we worked with. This was one of the benefits of working at the same place and being married. A strong family is one that stays close and supports each other. I wonder why God's Love Institute doesn't understand that yet...

The other staff told me that the girl's units are probably worse then the boy's units because the girls physically fight more than the boys. When one of the units on campus gets really out of hand, that unit will get on the intercom and say "Code Red, Code Red". When the other units hear that, then all the available staff rapidly respond to that unit to help out. The other staff says that the majority of the "Code Reds" comes from the girl's units. The girls are either fighting each other or destroying company property...

Usually all the men respond to these Code Reds because the girls seem too settled down faster when they see several 200 pound men running through the door of the unit. From what I hear, the girls units are out of control and that comes from poor supervision. I guess Janet will be finding out soon enough because she is going to working at the girl's unit. I'm sure she will have some stories to tell me at the end of every shift. I hope the staff that she works with isn't as bad as the staff I've met so far in the boys units. At least right now, God's Love Institute has two people who give a damn about the kids and they are Janet and myself. I know there are more; I just have not met them yet. I going to keep thinking positive because I know God will be working on this situation for me...

Janet's supervisors' name is Miss Ronda; she has been working for God's Love Institute for 20 years. From what other staff says, she is very laid back and lets the staff do what ever they want at the units. A lot of staff believes that she is just too burned out to give a damn anymore. I guess she fits right in with some of the other supervisors here on campus. Miss Ronda is in her early 40's, but she looks like she is in her 50's. She looks like she's lived a very stressful life. She has an eight-year-old daughter who is a confirmed brat from what I hear. Miss Ronda gives her everything she asks for, I guess she is a burned out parent to. Hopefully Janet won't have any problems working with Miss Ronda...

Janet was happy to find out that there were only six girls that lived at her unit. None of the girls liked Miss Ronda for an assortment of reasons. All the girls told their stories about how Miss Ronda lied to them on several occasions. The problem with these lies is that they would make the girls very upset and they usually would take it out on the nearest staff. The girls would be physically or verbally abusive to the staff and they didn't do anything but show up for work. Since Miss Ronda wasn't there on the units after she told the kids lies, it only made sense for them to take their anger out on the staff. Janet knew that this was something that she would have to deal with some day. A person like Miss Ronda was called a "Fire Starter"; this is a person who creates problems with the kids and the staff has to try and resolve the problem. Janet knew that working with the kids would be a lot easier if wasn't for the damn Fire starters on campus...

That next Friday on my 3-11 shifts, I asked Mr. Curly where the iron was because I didn't see it anywhere on the unit. Usually the kids ask to iron their clothes on Saturday mornings so I wanted to know if it was broke. The iron is normally sitting on the ironing board in the hallway upstairs. It has been there faithfully every since I started working here and now it's gone. Mr. Curly said with an angry look on his face, "It's locked up in the closet for safety reasons". Out of curiosity, I asked him what happened. He said, "Last night when I was upstairs sitting in the hall, someone threw the iron at me. It just missed my head by inches, I was very fortunate"...

I said, "Do you know who threw it?" He said, "I was working overtime, it was about 1:00am and all the kids were suppose to be asleep. All I know is it come from that end of the hallway". He was pointing towards where eight kids sleep and Amos was one of the kids. I said, "So it could be anyone down that end of the hall who threw the iron". None of the kids liked Mr. Curly so it really could be anyone of them. It could probably be any kid on campus because I hear that he has done some bad things to these kids. If you treat someone bad, it usually comes back to haunt you later on. Probably all the kids at St. Pauls put a plan together to bust him upset his big ass head with that iron...

Deep down inside, I was wishing that Mr. Curly would have got hit by that iron; he certainly earned it after all the years of abusing the kids. I wish I could have been there to see the dumbass look on his face when that iron came flying pass his big shiny bald head. Mr. Curly told me that all the kids were on restriction until someone confessed to the incident. I personally didn't think that punishment was fair because only one kid threw the iron. All the kids simply shouldn't be punished for what one kid did. These kids aren't in the Military; there shouldn't be "Corporal Punishment" to try to resolve a problem. This is a situation when the supervisor should step in and do something about this. At least that's what I think a good supervisor should do. I guess the key word in what I just said is "good supervisor". Are there any good supervisors on this campus? A good supervisor could put a stop to a lot of this bullshit that goes on at God's Love Institute...

I'm so happy that I only have to work with this idiot (Mr. Curly) once a week. If I had to work with him every day I would probably quit or punch him in the mouth. All the other staff was okay with the way he handled the iron throwing incident. That is because they are all followers; this just gave them another excuse to treat the kids bad. The only things the kids were allowed to do this week was eating and going to the campus Church on Sunday. That is where I met the Spiritual Advisor on campus "Mr. Douglas", a white 50 year old male who has been working for God's Love Institute for 20 years. He started out working at the units with Mr. Derek as a Primary Youth Counselor. Ten years ago he went back to college and got his Master's degree in Theology and that is when God's Love Institute created the position of Spiritual Advisor. The staff at my unit always tries to find an excuse to not take the kids to church on Sundays, but not me. I always took a couple a kids to Church every Sunday because I believe in the power of God...

After Church one Sunday, Mr. Douglas introduced himself to me. He said with a big smile on his face, "I'm Mr. Douglas and I just want to thank you for bringing the kids to Church every Sunday. This is the most that St. Pauls has been here in a year". I smiled and said, "Your welcome, these kids need God in their lives and so do the staff". He said, "Before you came to the unit, the staff always had some excuse why they couldn't bring the kids to Church. This was becoming very frustrating for me and no one was doing anything about this problem. I said, "Well as long as I'm working on Sundays, I'll always bring as many kids as I can to Church". He said, "Thank you Mr. Renaldo, you're a good man. Bless you, I wish more staff were like you". I shook his hand and got my kids together to take them back to the unit to eat some lunch...

It was a breath of fresh air to meet Mr. Douglas after dealing with all these idiots. Now I know someone other than Janet and me who gives a damn about the kids. It took me six months to find a good person like him, but after meeting Mr. Douglas it was worth the wait. He is a "Teacher of the heart and an educator of the mind". He preaches the love of God and that is (in my opinion) the foundation of hope for troubled youth today. These kids have been let down by so many self consumed mothers and fathers, but Mr. Douglas tells them that God will never let them down. Hopefully if the staff can do a better job of getting the kids to Church so they can hear these words of love and hope from Mr. Douglas; the more the kids will start to understand and believe in God...

I was a troubled youth growing up and I know that if it was not for the "Grace of God" I wouldn't be alive today. I understand what some of these kids are going through and I can relate. This is why I take my job so seriously, I feel their pain all way down to my soul. I believe in my heart that God has sent me to God's Love Institute to help these kids in some way. Ten years ago, all I wanted was to make a million dollars. Now all I want is to make a positive difference in these kids' lives. I know I can, I just have to be patience and wait for the answers from God. I have to keep my eye on the big picture, which is helping the kids to have a loving and caring environment. So I'll continue to pray and do the best job that I can in spite of the idiot staff that I have to work with... **<u>"Believe in Change"</u>**

Chapter 7

"The Promotion"

One day, Mr. Kojak (Assistance Supervisor) approached me and asked me if I wanted to be the Assistance Supervisor. I thought he was joking at first because I haven't been here that long. He told me that he wants to take another position as a "Clinical Case Manager". He says with a smile on his face, "I think you would make a great supervisor because you are a professional and you get along well with the kids". Without given it much thought I told him that he could put my name in for the job; I would like to give the job a shot and see if it works for me. He said, "I'm going to tell Mr. Derek that you are interested and he should be getting in touch with you very soon". Out of curiosity I asked Mr. Kojak how much longer he was going to be the supervisor. He said, "Probably about one more month; I'm looking forward to doing something else". I told him good luck and thanked him for considering me for the position. He smiled and said, "You are the best man for the job in my opinion". He shook my hand and walked away…

Later on that night I told Janet about me being offered the supervisor's position. She was excited at first and then she began to think about me dealing with that worthless Mr. Derek. He is a man known for not doing shit, except dressing good and running his mouth. None of those qualities has anything to do with getting the job done. I began to seriously second-guess myself now. Can I really work for a man who doesn't give a fuck about nothing but how good he looks? I'm already working for him now; at least if I get the job I can hopefully make some positive changes for the kids. So how bad can it be? If I can't make a positive difference, then I will just abdicate myself from the position. I'll just go back to being a Primary Youth Counselor. Janet told me that she would support whatever decision I made. She always has my back and that's why I love her so much...

Normally a person had to have a Bachelors' Degree to even be considered for the position of Assistance Supervisor on any unit. I guess I should be honored to even be considered without having my degree. It wasn't long before I talked to Mr. Derek and he told me that the company might make an exception for me because I was only a year away from getting my Degree in Child Psychology. I already had an Associates' Degree in "Child and Family Studies"...

Mr. Derek told me that the final decision wasn't up to him. His boss, Miss Lisa, the Director of Residential Living had the final say on the matter. She is a 50 year old Italian lady who has been working for the company for over 20 stressful years. The word on her from the other staff is that she is also burned out. Now she just basically walks around campus looking good with her long black curly hair hanging down her back. The rumor is that Miss Lisa and Mr. Derek are lovers and she faithfully does anything he wants. Staff says that she is the reason that Mr. Derek gets away without doing any work. When I see them together is obvious that something more than a work relationship is going on. You can see it in their eyes and the way they touch each other when they talk. They always look like two high school sweethearts who are trying to hide their relationship from their parents. This would be cute if it didn't affect the quality of help the children were getting...

Mr. Larry found out about the Assistance Supervisor's position and decided to apply for the job. Mr. Larry says that he has a Degree in Criminal Justice, but the other staff says that he just lies about having a degree. He is really a college dropout and too ashamed to be honest about it. When I found out that he was applying for the position, I told him good luck and may the best man win. I don't think he would make a good supervisor, but I didn't want him to know what I was thinking. I really wanted to tell him, "You're an idiot and shouldn't be anywhere close to a child". Janet is the only one who knows what's on my mind because there's no one at this job that I trust yet. It would be absolutely criminal to put him in a position that has more power than he has right now. Nothing here surprises me anymore, but I think even that would shock me...

A month passed and still no mention from Mr. Derek who was going to get the supervisor's position. Everyday Mr. Larry asked me if I heard anything yet and I constantly told him the same thing, "No, if I hear something you'll be the first to know". Mr. Kojak had already moved into his new position and now St. Pauls doesn't have an Assistance Supervisor. We have to direct any problems to Mr. Derek and it may be days before the staff gets a response back from him. This is no way to run a unit that deals with troubled kids. The staff says that Mr. Derek has always been like this so I might as well get use to waiting. We shouldn't have to get use to this bullshit from Mr. Derek. Maybe if I get the supervisor's job I can make this situation better. At least that's my plan anyway; I have to remain positive...

Six weeks after I put in for the position Mr. Derek secretively told me that it looks like I'm going to get the job. He said, "Everything is looking good, we just have to cross all the T's and put the paper together. So it shouldn't be too much longer now Mr. Renaldo". I told him, "Thank you for considering me for the job". He said, "Don't say anything to anyone else yet until I get the final word from Miss Lisa" I told him okay and shook his hand firmly wondering if I could find a pulse from his heart somewhere. Sometimes I really feel like there is no soul inside this man when I'm near him...

Thinking back on the whole conversation; I don't remember him making any eye contact with me. All the time he was talking to me he was looking away from me as if he had something to hide. It is hard to trust a person who can't even briefly look me in the eyes. It was like he was waiting for a bolt of lightning to strike him down. Dealing with him is always like

51

making a drug deal. Mr. Derek is always so secretive and sneaky and I'm never sure why. Everyone on campus says the same thing about him. Maybe someday I'll get used to the way he acts...

On a Saturday afternoon around two o'clock, we took all the kids outside to get some fresh air. Some of the kids were teasing each other and they began to get angry with each other. It is one of St. Paul's kids named Jeremiah that is involved in this argument. He is a big muscled-bound kid who loves to show off to the other kids, especially when he is at the gym lifting weights. He is an African American male, 17 years old and has plans to go into the Marines when he gets his discharge from God's Love Institute. Most of the time, he is no trouble for the staff and a pleasure to be around. Today a kid named Malachi from Obadiah Hall was able to get deeply under his skin. Malachi is a skinny, 17 year old white male, who would be physically crushed if Jeremiah grabbed him and started beating his ass...

The kids from Obadiah Hall are allowed to do whatever they want to because their staff is assholes and don't care. Most of time, the staff don't even come out of the unit to watch the kids. On many occasions you can see the staff peeking out the window occasionally to see if the kids are okay...

Mr. Jackson approached Jeremiah and told him that he had to go inside the unit because of all the cursing he was doing. I agreed with Mr. Jackson when he told me that he was going to take Jeremiah inside because it looked like he was ready to kill Malachi. None of the staff from Obadiah Hall said anything to Malachi about his negative behavior. I wasn't happy with the fact that not one of Malachi's staff said anything to him. As a matter of fact there wasn't even one of his staff in the area. I went over with Mr. Jackson and I told Malachi that he had to go to where his staff was...

Some of his staff is sitting on benches nowhere near their kids, socializing as if they didn't have any kids to supervise.

Malachi didn't say anything; he just slowly turned and walked away with a smile on his face. Mr. Jackson told Jeremiah again in a stern voice, "You need to come with me right now" as he walked closer to him. Jeremiah angrily said, "Why do I have to go inside and nothing happens to that fucking Malachi? Mr. Jackson said, "He's not one of St. Paul's kids so I have no control over what happens to him". Jeremiah said, "This is some bullshit" and he started walking slowly towards the unit. Once he got inside, he sat down on the bench outside the staff's office quietly mumbling obscenities...

A few minutes later, Mr. Moe and Mr. Larry brought the rest of the kids inside. I thought this was a bad idea because kids tend to act-out more when there is an audience of their peers present. Jeremiah started talking and cursing loudly about how he didn't think it was fair that he was the only one who had to come inside. Now he had a crowd of his peers to encourage his bad behavior and that is like adding fuel to the fire...

Mr. Jackson told him to come upstairs with him as he gently nudges his arm. Jeremiah says in a hostile voice, "Why do I have to go upstairs?" Mr. Jackson says angrily, "Because I told you to". He reaches out and then grabs his arm forcefully to escort him upstairs. Jeremiah tightens up his body to resist the potential physical restraint that usually comes from the staff in incidents like this. Mr. Jackson tugs on his arm as if he was pulling on a heavy door open. Seeing that Mr. Jackson is getting no where with Jeremiah, I decided to go over to assist him. I grabbed his other arm tightly, but he just tightened up even more. His eyes begin to fill with tears and fear as the constant anticipation of a restraint began to overwhelm him. He started sweating as if the temperature in the room had suddenly gone up 30 degrees making it well over 110°. I couldn't tell if Jeremiah was reacting this way because of anger or fear. I just knew the situation was becoming even more volatile as each minute passed...

I tried talking to Jeremiah, but he didn't seem to hear or acknowledge a single word that I said. Mr. Moe wisely took all the other kids into the T.V. room because it would be easier to work with Jeremiah if they aren't around. The kids moaned and groaned, but finally they went with him. Mr. Moe told Mr. Jackson to go watch the kids in the TV room while he went to deal with Jeremiah. Mr. Moe told Jeremiah in a high piercing voice, "I'm tired of fucking with you and now it's time to go upstairs". I leaned over and told Jeremiah in a calm voice that we could talk about the situation more upstairs in private. I spoke in a low calming voice with the hope that he would respond to that better than Mr. Moe shouting at him. He looked at me with a defeated look on his face and said in a soft voice, "Okay Mr. Renaldo, but I still don't think this is fair". He stood up slowly as me and Mr. Moe watched closely. Not sure if he was going to run or fight, we mentally prepared ourselves for the worse scenario…

Jeremiah slowly started walking down the hall and up the stairs; everything was going according to plan. My plan is to get Jeremiah to his room without a restraint. When he got to the stairs, he started cursing loudly again. Mr. Moe said in a frustrated voice, "You young motherfuckers aren't going to be talking to me like that, so you better shut the fuck up". I personally didn't care what Jeremiah said, just as long as he was still walking towards his room. I didn't see anything wrong with the way he was venting because I knew there could be worst things he could be doing right now. He could be fighting, breaking things or assaulting the staff; we should be ecstatic that he is just verbally venting. No one gets any cuts or bruises from just simple words. This was Jeremiah's way of regulating his anger and we should be congratulating him for showing this kind of control. These kids come from very violent backgrounds, so this was actually a step forward for him. If only the other staff understood what was really going on with this kid right now…

Out of nowhere like a thunderous bull, Mr. Moe turns and forcefully slams Jeremiah against the wall. He attempts to fight back, but Mr. Moe is much too strong for him. He violently slams Jeremiah down to the floor like a professional wrestler and begins to choke him. I'm in shock because this was the last thing that I expected since the kid was doing what we asked him to do. We were only ten feet from Jeremiah's room so why would Mr. Moe start a restraint. This didn't make any damn sense to me; what a fucking idiot! I guess Mr. Moe's poor little ego was rubbed the wrong way. All Jeremiah was doing was running his mouth, which is no reason to restrain a kid. I rushed over to make sure Mr. Moe didn't try to kill Jeremiah. I firmly grabbed Mr. Moe and told him to hold Jeremiah's arm. I grabbed the other arm as Jeremiah apparently resisted more in fear than retaliation. Now tears are flowing from Jeremiah's eyes onto the floor where we have his face firmly smashed against the hard cold tile... **"Believe in Change"**

Chapter 8

"The Staff's Role Model"

Mr. Jackson came running upstairs after hearing all the noise we were making. Mr. Larry stayed downstairs to watch the other kids to make sure they didn't get into any trouble. Mr. Jackson grabbed Jeremiah's legs to stop them from flailing around. Mr. Moe said, "Mr. Jackson, hold his arm and let me get his legs". Mr. Moe quickly stood up holding his head, looking and feeling for blood with his fingers. He must have banged his head against the wall when he slammed Jeremiah against it. There was a large red bump the size of a fifty cent piece, above his right eye making him look like he was in a 10 round boxing match. He said furiously, "You motherfucker, there's a bump on my head; now I'm really going to fuck you up"…

He forcefully grabbed both Jeremiah's legs and applied all his weight on them. He didn't care what kind of possible damage that might occur by doing this. Then he slowly presses them firmly up towards the middle of Jeremiah's quivering back. He screamed loudly in pain as Mr. Moe pressed harder on his legs as if he wanted them to break. I was waiting for the rare sound of breaking bones to come to my ears. That would have really fucked me up mentally to hear that sound. I'm not sure what I would have done if I did hear bones breaking. These violent restraints are so primitive and unnecessary. I guess as long as we continue to do restraints anything is possible, including death. It was probably a good thing that Jeremiah was a big strong kid and in good physical shape. If he wasn't in shape I believe some of his bones would have broken…

Jeremiah stopped screaming as if his body went numb and his breathing began erratic and shallow. Jeremiah's asthma had raised its ugly head to steal the air from his lungs again. He was no longer resisting the pressure against his legs, but that didn't stop Mr. Moe from diligently putting more pressure on them. He was like a mad man on Jeremiah's legs, I wasn't sure if he wasn't really crazy or temporarily insane. I wasn't sure if he would be happy if he didn't get to break something today. Mr. Moe had to hear the wheezing sounds coming from Jeremiah's throat, but he just didn't give a damn...

I began to calmly talk to Jeremiah about trying to control his breathing, but it wasn't working. Especially since a 320 pound idiot was trying to break both his knees. I told Mr. Moe that Jeremiah was having trouble breathing and he needed to stop. He didn't say anything at first and then he finally slowly got off of Jeremiah's legs. Mr. Moe was sweating profusely like he had just run five miles in 90 degree weather. I thought that I would have to kick him off Jeremiah's legs if he didn't move faster. There is something seriously wrong with Mr. Moe that leads me to believe he really does need a therapist. He definitely has psychological issues that need to be addressed before he kills one of these poor kids...

I told everyone to back up and give Jeremiah some room to breathe because the air was real thick in the hallway. He didn't move at all, he just laid there defeated and his body was physically begging for air. I needed some fresh air myself because I was hot and sweaty. I was physically and psychologically drained from dealing with this situation. I felt like I was also in a 10 round fight. I told Jeremiah to take some deep breaths and begin to physically demonstrate to him how. He started imitating what I was doing right away like an infant just learning a new skill. His breathing was beginning to get better and after ten minutes he was able to get up and walk to his room with a little assistance from me. He flopped on his bed in exhaustion as I turned to leave his room. I told him that I would talk to him later after he gets some rest...

After the adrenaline of the restraint started to abate, I noticed a sharp burning pain in my right elbow. I grabbed it to feel for blood. I saw a little blood on my fingers, so I looked in a mirror in the bathroom to see what was going on. I saw that all the skin was scraped off my elbow down to the white meat. It looked bad and it hurt like hell. There was a large abrasion, about two inches wide and three inches long above my elbow. I reluctantly ran some water on the wound to clean it. It burned like hell when the water touched it, but I expected that. I almost screamed out loud, but I caught myself. I found some gauze and covered it up to protect it from germs. Now I'm really pissed off at Mr. Moe for getting me involved with this unnecessary bullshit restraint. He has a bump on his head and Mr. Jackson has a pain in his lower back. We had to go through all of this because Mr. Moe's ego was rubbed the wrong way. It is amazing what pain one idiot can bring on others. This just isn't right!!!

Mr. Moe said that he would stay upstairs with Jeremiah so that Mr. Jackson and I could take a much-needed break downstairs. I asked Mr. Moe was he going to do the paperwork for the restraint. He smiled and said that he would take care of it later. I wasn't sure how he was going to write the restraint up because it really was unnecessary and avoidable. Mr. Moe could have just let Jeremiah run his mouth to vent and nothing would have happened. I guess there was too much ego involved for that to happen...

In my opinion, most restraints are because some of the staff get their egos' hurt and retaliate by doing a restraint on the kid. I guess that is what happens when you hire an employee and don't train them properly. I also think that there should be some kind of psychological evaluation prior to hiring anyone. Even a person with an education should have one, but I guess someone would have to give a damn first...

A week later, I still haven't heard anything about the paperwork on Jeremiah's restraint. I didn't want to make any waves yet, so I didn't ask about it again. No one asked me about the restraint, not even Mr. Kojak. It was like the restraint never happened; except for the scar on my elbow, which is taking its good old time healing. I also have my trusted notebook that I can always refer to if I had to recall what happened in the restraint. I can see now that a lot of paperwork never gets written, especially if it's about the staff abusing the children. I know management doesn't want this information to get out to the public. They better hope that I never decide to write a book about this shit and get someone to read it. There is no way the people who are in charge, don't know or haven't heard about the abuse the staff do to these poor kids. How are these so called religious people able to sleep at night when the spirits of these children are being destroyed daily? What kind of nuns would run a place like this? Can money really change a person that much? I believe it would have to be a combination of the devil and the desire to make money to make this kind of change in this organization...

One day on a Friday shift, we had all the St.Pauls boys outside in the field. About 50 feet from the unit, there is a large field that the kids use to play football, baseball or run the quarter mile track. Right next to that is a small basketball playing area that the kids also enjoy using. This is where everyone takes the kids when they need to burn off built up energy from being in the units all day. The field is surrounded by benches where the staff usually sits and socializes while the kids are outside. The kids also use this opportunity to socialize with the other units, particularly the girl's units. It is a policy at God's Love Institute not to let the boys and girls mingle. This is to keep down any drama that could possibly happen between two horny teenagers. Of course if there is a horny teenager, they will find a way to make contact with each other. Most of the time the staff aren't paying attention to the kids or just don't give a damn. I'm trying to keep an eye on all our kids, but that is almost impossible for one person to do. All the other staff is just sitting around laughing and joking with each other. This job would be so much simpler if I was like the other staff and just didn't give a damn...

One of the girls named Esther starts arguing with one of St.Pauls kids named Jonah. Mr. Curly shouts and tells Jonah to get away from the girl. The girl follows him around the field cursing loudly and threatening to hit Jonah with a tree limb that she picked up. Mr. Curly tells him to come to where he is sitting, but Esther also follows him there. Her staff is nowhere to be found to even try to redirect Esther's negative behavior. Jonah calmly sits down next to Mr. Curly and smiles. Esther is still threatening to bust him in the head with the tree limb. I expected Esther to stop after Jonah sat down next to Mr. Curly, but she just didn't give a damn. He firmly told Esther that she needed to go where her staff was before she gets in trouble. She looks at him and loudly says, "What and the hell are you going to do old man". Mr. Curly tells her again as he quickly stands up, "You better get away from here; I'm not putting up with your foolishness today". Esther points her finger towards Mr. Curly's face and says, "What in the hell you going to do, you fucking old ass man?" Now I can feel the growing tension in the air as the crowd of staff and kids starts to gather. It was like the quiet before the storm and Mr. Curly was the unpredictable storm...

Mr. Curly says loudly (voice much deeper and serious now), "Don't put your finger in face because I will break it off". Finally Esther's staff (Miss Angela and Miss Lois) approached from where ever they been sitting to redirect her, but it is too late now. She is not willing to listen to anyone now and continues her constant threats towards Mr. Curly. She doesn't even care about hitting Jonah anymore; all her attention and anger is focused directly towards Mr. Curly now. Esther's staff may have had a chance to calm her down if they would have talked to her when this first started. She is definitely too angry now to listen to anyone. Most of the kids here have a problem with self-regulation and she is one of the main ones. When Esther gets started it almost always ends up in a restraint on her. Miss Angela and Miss Lois are literally pleading with Esther to come with them. It is like she couldn't hear them or the staff were speaking a foreign language to her...

There was no turning back for Esther now; someone is going to have to restrain her. Even her face looked distorted from the anger that showed its ugly head. Her eyes seemed have turned a light red and sweat was popping up all over her face like boiling water. Even her voice had got raspy and deep, as if she swallowed a ball of cotton. This is a big contrast from the angelic look that is usually on her face. It is amazing the affect anger can have on a person's expression. I guess I could say the staff has the same problem controlling their feelings also because they have trouble with regulating their emotions. Esther quickly steps closer to Mr. Curly and firmly presses her finger on the side of his face and says, "What the fuck you going to do, you fucking blind old ass man?" Now everyone is in shock over the boldness of this little girl's negative actions and words towards staff...

Mr. Curly looked around as if trying to see if anyone of importance was in the area. With one quick calculated move like a ninja, he grabbed Esther's finger off his face and viciously snapped it backwards and calmly sat down. I could hear the eerie snapping sound of the bone in her finger. It sounded like a small tree limb breaking in half. Esther screamed in uncontrollable pain as she sank down to her knees like a deflated balloon. Mr. Curly just sat there with a smile on his face, confidently staring at her. Everyone outside came running towards Esther to see how bad she was hurt. Mr. Curly jumps up and says loudly, "I had no choice, she tried to attack me. I had to defend myself; we can't let these damn kids attack staff". Miss Angela picked Esther up from the ground to look at her finger...

Her finger was bent in the opposite direction and I could see the bone sticking out as blood dripped from it. Mr. Curly seen the finger and said, "She must have broke her finger when she hit the ground". I told that child that she wasn't allowed to assault staff, but she wouldn't listen". I could hear the other staff saying to each other, "Hey, she brought it on herself by putting her hands on Mr. Curly. We can't let these kids run us, we have to defend ourselves. We got your back Mr. Curly". These comments were coming from all the cheerleading male staff; the women staff didn't say anything because they were still in shock...

Esther looked at Mr. Curly and said, "That old motherfucker broke my finger and I'm going to tell my Mom". Of course Esther's mom doesn't give a fuck or she would be raising her child right now. Her mother is a drug addict and living on the streets waiting on her next hit of crack cocaine. Miss Angela grabbed Esther's arm and started walking her toward their unit. There was no resistance from Esther now; she had no more fight left in her. She hobbled along like a broken stallion that had no more fight left inside. She didn't want anything else to do with Mr. Curly that day. I could hear Esther crying with each step she made. I felt a sorrow run through my body, this was a feeling I never felt before. I felt like I just witness a child's murder and there was nothing I could do about it. Another young spirit has been destroyed by that demon named Mr. Curly...

Mr. Curly just sat there with a half-smile on his face; it was like he was in a trance. There was a look of satisfaction on his face that really disgusted me. Jonah was still sitting next to him with his head down. I could tell he wasn't happy after watching Esther get hurt. Even though Jonah and Esther had been arguing, he still didn't want to see her get hurt like that. This man should be arrested and put in jail, but I don't expect that to happen. The company will probably cover this up also and that will be the end of the whole event...

I could hear the other staff proudly talking among themselves saying, "Those kids should no better than to mess with Mr. Curly because he has been fucking these kid up for years". I thought to myself: This is so sad that a person like Mr. Curly is honored and revered by the other staff on this campus...

He is feared by children of all ages, all races and sexual orientation. He is the "king of abusers", what an honorable title to have next to your name. The staff talk about Mr. Curly like he is a superstar and everyone wants to be like him. He is allowed to abuse children with no obvious fear of going to prison or getting fired. I believe children are very special to God and Mr. Curly will have to answer to him one day. What kind of person would use him as a role model except for some of the staff at God's Love Institute? This is so sad... **<u>Believe in Change</u>**

Chapter 9

"The Mentally of Abuse"

a week later I saw poor little Esther with a cast on her hand and looking very sad. She just put her head down as she walked pass the front porch of St.Pauls. I hollered to her to say hi, but she just kept looking at the ground as if she had dropped something. She actually started walking faster after she heard me, as if something scary suddenly appeared behind her. Maybe it was the memory of being abuse by Mr. Curly that suddenly started mentally following her down the sidewalk. Miss Angela waved to me as she hurried to keep up with Esther, who was walking even faster now. When I first met Esther, she had the spirits of fire and strength inside of her. Now I don't sense any spirit in her young body. She has all the signs of a child whose spirit has been broken or destroyed. Just like her finger was broken, so was her heart and soul. She quickly ran down the sidewalk trying to get away from her emotional demons of abuse…

I wonder how many souls or spirits Mr. Curly has destroyed and then claimed as a trophy to brag about to the other staff. He is like a dangerous demon among unsuspecting angels, living and striving off the misery of poor innocent children. I felt like a part of my spirit was gone after witnessing the abuse of this poor child and the company not doing anything about it. Believe it or not, nothing ever did happen to Mr. Curly from this company for what he did to Esther. It is still secretively talked about among the staff as they sit around eating their lunches. There wasn't even an informal investigation of Mr. Curly………

Not one single staff was interviewed or questioned about what happened that day. I know this man must feel incredibly invincible now, especially after breaking a child's finger and nothing happens to him. He should be in prison with inmates who hate men like him; I wonder how tough he would be then. I wrote a statement about what I saw and gave it to Mr. Derek, but I never got a response to it. I kept a copy for my records so that I could have some evidence that I did say something about it. I will still have my notes to fall back on if someone finally does give a damn...

The abuse of children seems to be a way of life at this job considering how long it's been going on. How are these children ever going to be able to trust or respect adults after dealing with this bullshit at God's Love Institute. The future of these children is very bleak because of what they are learning here will not have a damn thing to do with them making it in this world. Hopefully if I get the supervisor's position I can make some positive changes. I would start by firing that child abuser Mr. Curly the first chance I get. I just can't figure out why he hasn't been fired yet; how is this possible? This man is extremely psychotic and needs help from a professional therapist. Why is this company turning its back to what's going on in the units? Management stays in their soft plush office chairs and never come out to the units to see what is really going on. Maybe that helps them sleep at nights...

If the people at the Main building did come to the units they would hear the horror stories from the kids'. Maybe they would do something about the abuse. They are like the "Slave-Masters" sitting in the big mansion waiting for the cotton to be picked by the staff. There is only one African American who works in the Main Building, which is where all the big shots work. He is the Executive Director of Residential Living; his name is Mr. Bojangles. He looks more like a white man, than he does a Black man. He is very light skinned with black wavy hair. He could very easily pass for a white man with a sun tan. I have never seen him on the units. The majority of the staff on the units is African American (95%). My impression of him is that he is the "House nigger" and "Yes man" for the company. Since the majority of children at God's Love Institute are African American, this makes sense to have a black face in a position of apparent power at the Main building...

One day on the weekend while we were upstairs, Mr. Larry was having a problem with Jonah. He wouldn't listen to any of Mr. Larry's redirections. Jonah was in one of his unpredictable moods. Mr. Larry was getting very angry and Jonah could tell by the way he was acting. The worse thing a staff could do is let a kid know that he is getting to them. In my opinion all this does is encourage the negative behavior. A kid like Jonah who comes straight from the city streets, will eat that situation up. I told Mr. Larry that I was going to take Jonah downstairs to calm down in the "Quiet-room". This is a padded room set up to let the child vent without disrupting the routine of the other children in the unit. It is a 10x10 room with no windows; it is right next to the staff's office. Most restraints occur in route to the Quiet-room so I have to be very careful not to get in Jonah's personal space. When we calmly walked pass Mr. Larry, Jonah didn't say anything to him. Mr. Larry said loudly, "You're lucky because I was getting ready to fuck you up"...

Jonah quickly turned towards Mr. Larry saying, "Well come on motherfucker, I'm not scared of you, let's do it". Mr. Larry stood up slowly saying, "You're not going to be talking to me like that". Then he violently grabbed and forcefully slammed Jonah to the floor with all the power he had from all the years of lifting weights. Jonah tried to fight back, but Mr. Larry was just too strong for him. To make sure Mr. Larry didn't hurt him to bad, I decided to help him control Jonah by holding his arm. Instead of Mr. Larry holding the other arm, he quickly grabbed one of Jonah's legs and meticulously bends it up towards the center of his back. Jonah moans in pain as both his legs are pressed towards the center of his back...

Apparently Mr. Larry must do this move a lot because he did it with the precision of a professional wrestler. I reached over to hold the other arm so Jonah couldn't punch me in the face. I didn't care if he punched Larry in his head because he sure did deserve it...

Jonah started screaming loudly in pain and I wasn't sure why because it seemed to come out of nowhere. I quickly turned around to see what Larry was doing to him to make him scream like that. I was amazed at what I saw this professional child abuser doing. He had taken Jonah's shoes and socks off and was sadistically bending all his toes back. I angrily said, "What in the hell do you think you're doing? You can't do that, are you trying to get both of us in trouble for doing an illegal restraint". He didn't stop at first as he struggled to hold Jonah's feet. He acted like he didn't hear me or he didn't care what I was saying. I wasn't sure if he was capable of stopping himself because there was a look of enjoyment on his face as Jonah continued to scream in pain. I shook him firmly on his shoulder to get his attention. I figured maybe he couldn't hear me with all the loud screaming that Jonah was doing. I told him again, "You better stop now or I'm leaving right now". Finally Mr. Larry stopped what he was doing to Jonah. Looking disappointed that I made him stop, he slowly stood up. He walked to the chair and sat down. I let Jonah lay there, hoping that we give him a chance to calm down...

After five minutes of listening to him moan in pain, I helped him up and walked him to his room. Jonah was limping badly as he slowly walked to the room. He looked like he was walking on hot burning coals with his bare feet. He sat on the edge of his bed with tears and sweat running profusely down his face. I felt bad for him; I wish I could do something to take his pain away. He just sat there staring at the wall as if he was in a trance. He was breathing deeply; he seemed to be trying to control his anger. He had the look of a crazy man or someone possessed by a demon. Uncertainty filled my thoughts; I wasn't sure what he was going to do next so I stayed alert for anything.

I was quiet and hardly moving as I sat on the bed across from him waiting for the next unpredictable move. He looked like he was trying to gather his energy from the air that he was breathing to attack someone. I hope he wasn't thinking about jumping on me because he won't be happy with the results. I'm not going to let any of these kids hurt me, especially since I'm not the one he's really angry with. If I thought I could get away with it, I would gladly help him beat Mr. Larry's ass; now that would be fun...

A few minutes later Mr. Larry came in the room. He started talking to Jonah in a sympathetic voice as if he really was concerned with how he was doing. Jonah didn't even look at him; he just sat there staring at the wall across the room. I told Mr. Larry that it would be best if he left the room for now because Jonah is not ready to talk right now. Mr. Larry said with a bemused look on his face, "Okay, I'll talk to him later". This man is simply a bucket of rocks to think that Jonah wants to talk to him after he almost broke all his toes. He has no idea how to work with these kids. Why would he think that Jonah would want to talk to him after he tried to inflict so much pain on him?

Later that day in the staff's office, I asked Mr. Larry what he was thinking about when he was bending that poor kid's toes back. He said smugly, "You have to show these kids who's in charge or they'll keep on fucking with you". I said, "I would appreciate it if you didn't do that kind of shit around me because I'm not down with that". He said with a blank look on his face, "Okay, but I'm telling you this is what you have to do in order to get respect around here". I said, "I was always told that if you want respect, you have to give respect". He says, "These kids don't know nothing about respect, didn't you see how he was talking to me upstairs". I could see that I wasn't getting anywhere with trying to educate this child abuser. He has been thinking this way too long and it is part of his behavior now. He is going to need therapy to help him and the majority of the other staff will also. This is a frustrating situation to deal with, but I need to be strong and think positive…

The only person that I could talk to about the abuse of the children was my wife. I was happy to have her to talk to because it would be too hard to keep these thoughts inside. I knew I couldn't keep all the craziness balled up inside without exploding or punching one of these retarded staff in the head. Janet told me the girl's units weren't much better. The female staff there was just as bad, if not worst as the men. The same abusive mentality was all over this campus like a black plague. The new employees learned from the veterans how to abuse the kids; what a vicious cycle this is and continues to be…

I'm starting to have trouble sleeping at night and I'm beginning to dread going to work. I am having nightmares about children being abused. I never had nightmares like that before until I start working at God's Love Institute. I should feel good about helping troubled youth, but I don't because of the people I work with. I feel like I should be doing more to help these children, but I'm not sure how to yet. I know quitting is not the answer for me because these kids need me. I know going to management won't do any good, so I'm going to be patient for now. I'll continue to pray about this situation because that is where I will find my answer…

One night after a shift (3-11), Mr. Larry and I were casually walking to our cars to go home. His car was parked next to mine in the parking lot outside of the unit. The closer we got to our cars, the stronger the smell of shit in the air got. I thought maybe he shit his pants or his breath was that bad, that's how strong the smell was. With the light from the street lamp, we could see something smeared on his windshield. It looked like mud, but is smelled like shit or raw sewage. Mr. Larry quickly went back in the unit to get some paper towels to swipe his windows clean. As he was wiping, the smell got even worse as he stirred some shit around on his windshield. Mr. Larry shouted loudly in anger, "Some motherfucker put shit on my fucking car. I'm going to kill some fucking asshole". He was pissed off and I couldn't blame him. I started laughing loudly in his face, I just couldn't control myself. I laughed so hard my side was hurting as I bent over in pain. This is the first time that I laughed at this job since I got hired. This is the first time I found anything to laugh about; I certainly needed this laugh...

Miss Amy, the staff from St. Johns heard me laughing and came outside. She smiled and said, "What wrong Larry, are you having a shity day?" She laughed loudly and quickly ran back into her unit. Mr. Larry said furiously, "That fucking bitch Amy did this to my car". I asked him why he thought that she did it. He said, "She is just paying me back because I pissed on her car one night after work last week. Miss Amy came back out and slowly walked over towards where we were standing. She had a big devilish smile on her face; she proudly said, "I pulled that shit out of the toilet just for you. I waited for one of the kids to take a big shit and grabbed it; I guess now we are even asshole"...

Mr. Larry angrily said, "You better get the fuck away from me before I rub your fucking face across my windshield". Miss Amy slowly backed up laughing hysterically loud and giving the middle finger to Mr. Larry with each step. He finished cleaning the shit off his windshield and he got in his car spinning wheels as he recklessly left the parking lot. He was obviously furious and embarrassed about the whole situation. I sat in my car thinking about what I just witness between these two staff. How crazy are these idiots that I work with to do something like this to each other. I have never heard anything so crazy before in my life. What kind of person would dig into a toilet to get some shit to rub on another person's car? These are the same people watching over the children at God's Love Institute. What chance do these children have to make it if they are being lead by such fools who believe playing in shit is fun? **"Believe in Change"**

Chapter 10

"A new sheriff in Town with no Power"

$\mathcal{M}$r. Derek called my house and told me that he had something very important to talk to me about. He asked me to come to work early (2:00pm) on my Friday shift. I wasn't sure what he wanted to talk about because there were so many things that had happened since the last time I talked to him. I figured it was about some of the restraints that had happened in my presence. He might even want to talk to me about getting the supervisors position. If he asks me about the restraints, I'll gladly tell him everything I have seen. I doubt if he does anything about it, but I'll tell him anyway. I have been waiting for someone to do something or at least investigate these situations on the units. I took all my notes about everything I saw and heard with me to the meeting. I wanted to give exact and precise details of everything that happened. Mr. Derek was late as he always is for meetings so I waited outside his office patiently. After 15 minutes of uncertainty, he finally showed up with that fake-ass smile on his face that he is known for...

I calmly said hello and shook his hand; then we went into his office to talk. He had a small stuffy office inside Obadiah Hall, which is a boy's unit. The office was only 10x10 in size, with a large dirty window that he could hardly look out at the parking lot in the back of the unit. There were papers carelessly thrown all over the floor. It looked like a hurricane had come through the room overnight. He had a lovely picture of his family on the wall which added some humanity to him. He had a very nice looking family; I was surprised because I never pictured him as a family man. He had two kids, a boy and girl, ages 14 (daughter) and 10 (son)...

I was amazed how sloppy his office was because of how
well dressed he always is. Apparently, he spent all his time
working on how he looked and not his office's appearance. He
smiled and said, "I got some good news for you Mr. Renaldo.
We (the company) are going to give you the supervisor's job.
There is just one stipulation to this promotion to supervisor. You
can keep it as long as you stay in college and get your degree.
No one has ever got this position without having at least a
Bachelors Degree as far as I can remember. You will be the first
one since I have been working for this company and I have been
here for over 15 years. There are a lot of people speaking very
highly of you, so don't let us down"…

I told him thanks and asked him when I can start the new
position. He said, "Well, you are the supervisor now, but I don't
want you to say anything about it to the other staff yet until I
announce it at the next team meeting next Tuesday (1:30 to
3:00pm)". He told me that the job was a salary position, so I
didn't have to use my time-card anymore to swipe in. My new
shift will be Monday through Friday 3:00pm to 11:00pm until he
hired more staff to cover that shift. Once he hired more staff, I
could work 1:00pm to 8:00pm Monday through Friday. I would
like that shift more because I could get a lot more done at home
and school…

I was happy because I didn't have to work on weekends
anymore when the average working person was off from work.
My wife will still be working the weekends and I will miss her.
My wife and I will figure something out later on how to get her
off for the weekends. If this new job puts me in a better position
to make life easier for these children, then it will be worth it to
me. I know my wife will understand because she knows how
important the welfare of the children is to us. Mr. Derek gave me
his cell phone number and shook my hand saying, "Give me a
call if you have any problems or questions"…

At the next team meeting Mr. Derek made an official announcement that I would be the new Unit Supervisor. He continued by saying, "All unit business should categorically go through Mr. Renaldo first, so if there are any problems you should contact him first. He will let me know what is going on and together as a team; we will work it out. I have the utmost confidence in Mr. Renaldo and I want you to feel the same way. While he was talking, I looked around the room to see the expressions on everyone's faces. Mr. Larry is the only one who had a look of disappointment on his face. He probably felt like he should have got the job because he has been working here longer. I know he is going to be even more of a problem now, but I expected him to be bitter if he didn't get the job. In two weeks I'll start my new job as the "New Sheriff" in town. I just hope that I have some guns (power) to back up this position...

Now coincidentally all the other staff are treating me even more differently. I guess now I'm really not one of the boys. I am part of management now and no one on campus trusts them. There are no casual conversations anymore and when I come around the staff stop talking as if they are frozen in time. There seems to be more tension in the air, I could feel it like the moisture of a hot humid summer day. No one knows how to deal with me because technically I'm still a Primary Youth Counselor and a Unit Supervisor until Mr. Derek hires more staff...

This position isn't going to work unless they hire someone soon. Staff doesn't want to work directly with a supervisor and I don't want to work directly with these staff until they separate the position. The staff needs to understand the distinct difference in the two positions of counselor and supervisor. This is the only way that the staff is going to respect me as a supervisor. It probably wouldn't make a difference anyway because I'm sure they would prefer not to have a supervisor at all so they can continue their abusive ways. Hopefully I won't have to be a counselor much longer and I can focus on being a good supervisor...

"Children on Layaway, it's all about the Money$$$"

Mr. Larry's uncle (Mr. Jerry) took my position on the weekends because he thought he could make more money. He worked 11:00pm to 7:00am for the last five years as a night shift worker. He took my position because he wanted to make more money and to work with different staff. There was a $1.50 an hour difference in pay working as a Primary Youth Counselor compared to working as a Night Worker. Mr. Jerry and Mr. Larry didn't get along with each other, I'm not sure why because Mr. Jerry is married to his aunt. I could tell by the way they acted when they saw and talked to each other. There seemed to be a lot of tension in the air when they were near each other...

Mr. Jerry always had something negative to say about Mr. Larry and he always has something bad to say about Mr. Jerry. He was the one who told me about Mr. Larry getting kicked out of the Marines and College. Mr. Jerry told me that Mr. Larry got kicked out of the Marines for selling drugs and flunked out of College because he was always high off of marijuana. Mr. Larry heard all the stories that Mr. Jerry was spreading around campus and it bothered him a lot. I guess he thought his uncle was disparaging his character...

Of course he didn't need his uncle to do that anyway because hardly anyone on campus thought he was worth a shit. He always said to me that he was going to punch his uncle in the middle of his fat ass chest. That is where Mr. Jerry had a life threatening open-heart surgery a few years ago. Hopefully one day they will kill each other because Mr. Jerry isn't worth a dime either. That will be a blessing for the children who have to be here to deal with these two idiots. The children wouldn't have to worry about those two abusing them anymore...

It is just amazing that a person like Mr. Jerry is still working at this place because I don't think he can get employment anywhere else. He must weigh at least 400 pounds and is only 5' 8", all that weight is around his humongous belly. He looks like he is about 50 years old with thinning black hair and wearing black pop bottle thick glasses that hang off his face.

74

The few unfortunate times that I did work with him, when he filled in on the weekends; I can honestly say that he isn't worth a dime...

When it comes to working with kids and other staff, he has no communicative skills at all. He acts like a miserable person who is here because he couldn't get a job anywhere else. I never know what's going to come out of the garbage disposal that he calls a mouth when me or the kids talks to him. What does that say about this company called "God's Love Institute" who actually hired this idiot. He is the worst kind of staff because he always starts problems with the kids that he can't handle. He doesn't know how or care about handling the problems that he starts. He always has the other staff do that for him and they are tired of doing his job. The staff calls him a "Fire Starter"; he starts problems with the kids and waits for the other staff to de-escalate the situation. The only time that he gets off his gigantic butt is for food and to use the bathroom a few times a shift...

There was only two steady staff working the 3-11 shifts and that is Mr. Curly and me. Everyone else is "fill-ins" that are working overtime and are just here for the extra money. Usually it is Mr. Moe and Mr. Stan that worked that shift (3:00pm-11:00pm) Monday through Friday with us. The two of them must work at least a hundred hours of overtime every week. I don't know why they needed so much money, but they hardly ever missed a day of work...

Most of the time Mr. Stan could hardly keep his eyes opened long enough to hold a conversation. There was times when he would fall asleep right in the middle of a sentence no matter what the subject was about. I really felt sorry for him because he seemed like a real nice person who's been overworked and underpaid for many years. Mr. Moe would be so irritable that he just treated the kids' bad all the time, especially the ones who didn't want to spend three hours lifting weights at the gym with him...

"Children on Layaway, it's all about the Money$$$"

I remember when I first met Mr. Moe at the unit before he knew what kind of person I was. He proudly said, "Where else can you make $40,000 a year for playing video games and lifting weights everyday". He's right; this is the perfect place to do it because no one cares about the kids at the main office building. This company must foolishly pay over a million dollars every year in overtime. Right now, there doesn't seem to be any end to the overtime that is available for the staff. All the company has to do is simply just pay more money to qualified professionals and these people would stay longer. These poor kids are never going to get the help they need if the staff are always overworked and underpaid. This is something that I have to put in God's hands because I don't know what to do right now to help these children... **"Believe in Change"**

Chapter 11

"Trying to make Changes"

Only 14 months after I started working at this job as a youth counselor and to my surprise, I'm a supervisor. I'm ready to make some positive changes, but I know that I need to take small positive steps first to accomplish this. The staff have been doing things their way so long that it is a learned behavior and this is going to take time to change. It would be a lot easier to fire all these staff. Then I could hire some new professional staff and teach them how to do the job the right way...

That would be too easy and I know my job isn't going to be easy because of the company that I work for. It is never easy to make positive changes when bad behavior has been running rampant for so long. What I have found is that most of the new staff, (Since I have been working here) has started off doing the right thing. After a few weeks they are changed by the veteran staff that poisoned their thinking. The new staff are so busy trying to be team players that they forget about the welfare of the children. They usually give in to the behaviors of the group of idiots (staff) who think their way is the right way...

After a few weeks of being a supervisor, I noticed that only a few staff was filling out the daily logs. The logs were always filled out in the past without any problems, but now there seems to be a problem. The daily logs are used to keep track of the behavioral progress of all the kids in the unit. This lets the on-coming shift be aware of any potential problems that the kids are having that day. At the end of each week the logs are added up by a point system (1-4) and the kid's level is determined for the next week...

The kid's level that week determines what they are allowed to do the following week. If the kid is on level one, than he/she isn't allowed to do anything, which I don't think is fair. Kids need activity to get rid of some of their negative energy in a positive way. The highest level gets to do more than the lower levels which sometimes causes a lot of problems on the units. This system really doesn't work because staff like Mr. Curly constantly abuses this system all the time. If he doesn't like a kid, he will always keep that kid on level one. He will even go as far as to change what another staff wrote in the daily logs. Hopefully I can do something about this abusive, unfair system of control that is called the level system...

The next time I saw Mr. Derek I asked him could I reprimand the staff who don't fill out the daily logs. He said, "I'll take care of it at the next team meeting". At the meeting he explained to the staff how important it was to fill out the daily logs. The staff doesn't really care what he says, so unfortunately nothing changed after the meeting. They don't have any respect for Mr. Derek because they know that he is all mouth and no action! If the staff is not going to listen to Mr. Derek, than why should they listen to me? This job is going to be a lot harder than I expected because I am going to need a support system to get anything done. This system of support has to come from management...

Everyday Mr. Curly comes to work late and no one says anything to him. I confronted him several times about it and he told me that he and Mr. Derek have an understanding about him coming late. He said, "I told Mr. Derek that sometimes I have to assist my wife with my mother-in-law because she is real sick". I asked Mr. Curly, "Do you have to help her everyday because you are late most of the time". He angrily said, "You can go talk to Mr. Derek, he will tell you about my situation". I told him okay and walked away, but I knew he was feeding me a bunch of bullshit. He is not the only staff who comes to work late, 90% of the campus staff comes to work late...

This is such an unprofessional environment, it's a damn shame this is allowed to go on. This has to be the worst organization that I have ever worked for in my life...

I began to think of ways to keep the kids active in a positively manner. I heard about a unit that didn't want their pool table anymore so I thought it would be a good idea to get a couple kids together and carry it up to our unit. Me and about four of the kids went down to the unit and brought the pool table back in pieces. Once we get the table back to the unit we all pitched in and put the table back together. All the kids were so proud of themselves for putting the table together and they did it as a team. All the kids were very excited about having a pool table in the unit...

All of the Three Stooges were against having a pool table at the unit because they thought it would be unsafe for kids to have access to pool sticks and pool balls. There shouldn't be any problem with kids shooting pool if the staff get up off their lazy asses and supervise them. I don't believe there was ever a safety issue; I just believe they looked at it as extra work for them. I took their concerns into consideration, but I thought the kids really needed a positive way to let out energy while they were in the unit...

I remember when I was a young troubled youth and how shooting pool used to always calm me down and make me feel better about life. I was hoping that this pool table would have the same effect on these children with my guidance and skill at shooting pool. The only thing the kids had to do in the unit is to watch TV and that is just a lot of sitting around. Children with their backgrounds need positive activities and I believe this fits that category...

One night, while I was preparing to go home after working a 3 to 11 shift, I notice the Three Stooges standing around the pool table in the dark as I was getting ready to leave. As soon as they saw me they became very quiet and one by one all three of them walked into the office without saying anything to me. I thought it was a little suspicious, but I was tired and ready to go home. I have gotten used to the Three Stooges plotting against me so it was no big deal so I figured that I would worry about them later...

When I came to work the next afternoon I discovered that the pool table was completely destroyed. I was very upset and I went to Mr. Derek's office to express myself. I told him that I thought it was the Three Stooges who took a knife and cut the table from one end to the other and viciously tore all the pockets out of the table. Mr. Derek said that he would investigate and let me know what he found out. I asked him would it be possible to get a new table for the unit and he quickly said no. He told me that the company didn't have that kind of money to spend on a pool table...

A few days later Mr. Derek told me that there was nothing he could do about the pool table and there was no concrete proof that Mr. Larry, Mr. Moe, and Mr. Curly had anything to do with destroying the pool table. I told Mr. Derek that even the kids know who destroyed the table because they heard Mr. Curly talking about it in the hallway. I also said that if we don't do something about this incident the kids are going to get mixed signals about what is right and what's wrong. Mr. Derek reiterated by saying there is simply nothing I can do about it because there is no proof of guilt. I don't even know why I wasted my time telling this idiot about this incident, I should have known he wasn't going to do anything about it...

This company needs some kind of dress code because most of the staff looks like they are homeless and live on the streets. Their clothes are torn and tattered; they don't look like they know what a bar of soap feels like. Some of the staff actually wears house slippers to work. I'm sure they would wear pajamas if they thought they could get away with it. On numerous occasions I have smelled foul odors coming from some of the staff, especially Mr. Moe and Mr. Jerry. It smelled like a combination of foot and ass that haven't been washed for a week. Some of the women aren't much better when it comes to their appearance. Not all of them, but most of them don't care what they look like. They wear a scarf and rollers in their hair or they just don't comb their hair at all. These are the same staff that are supposed to enforce dress codes on the kids. Why should the kids listen to someone who doesn't even care about how they look? The staff don't get paid a lot of money, but that is no excuse for looking like a bum when you come to work. Where is their pride in how they look and act?

Now months have passed and still I'm not able to make any positive changes in the unit. I can't get the staff to do something simple like the daily logs. I can't stop the unnecessary restraints unless I'm actually on a unit. I can't get the staff to come to work on time because I have no power to write them up. I can't get Mr. Derek to get off his lazy ass and help me because that would be like work...

God's Love Institute has not tried to hire any new staff to fill the shifts so I have to still work 3-11 everyday. I'm supposed to work a flexible schedule, but that won't happen until the unit gets some new staff...

Sometimes I would get called in to work on weekends to help fill a shift because a staff didn't show up for work. Most of the time staff didn't show up for work and didn't give the courtesy of notifying the staff on the unit. I couldn't count on having my weekends or holidays off and that sucks for me. I'm not getting paid enough money to put up with this bullshit on this unit. I don't know how much longer I can continue to do this without getting any help from management. I am not happy and life is too short to work at a place that doesn't make me happy. I guess being a unit supervisor will at least look good on my resume when I leave this ungodly place to find another job. This is so sad for me and the children...

Mr. Larry and Mr. Moe beat up one of the kids named Jonah after I went home one night. I left St. Pauls at 10:00pm and everything was nice and quiet. All the kids were in their beds or quietly reading a book. I didn't find out about the beating until the next day (1:00pm) from Mr. Derek on my home phone. He said, "How come you didn't tell me about the restraint on Jonah last night?" Confused, I asked him "What restraint, everything was quiet when I left at 10:00pm. What time did the restraint occur?" He said, "At about five or ten minutes after ten o'clock". I angrily said, "Mr. Larry or Mr. Moe didn't call me because if they did then I would have come back to the unit to help out. I wasn't even home yet when this occurred. I will definitely find out more about the restraint when I get to work today and I will let you know…"

When I got to the unit at 2:30pm, the Therapist named Miss Linda asked me did I know about the restraint of Jonah. I told her not until I got a call from Mr. Derek; Mr. Larry and Mr. Moe must have waited for me to leave before they beat the kid up. She said, "One of the other kids named Terry saw the whole thing from the doorway of his room. He said he saw Mr. Larry repeatedly kicking Jonah while Mr. Moe violently held him down. Jonah had to go to the emergency room because he had a dislocated shoulder from the restraint. Terry is willing to put the entire incident in writing". I happily said, "If Terry is willing to do that maybe I can get these two assholes fired this time". Miss Linda and I both wanted to get rid of the Three Stooges for a long time and couldn't get anyone from management to help us. She has been getting a lot of complaints from the kids, but nothing in writing to substantiate their stories…

The main character in most of the complaints is Mr. Curly, and then followed by Mr. Larry and Mr. Moe. I can call them (The Three Stooges) Moe, Larry and Curly, who are also very violent TV characters if you watch them on television. Miss Linda has been taking the complaints to Mr. Derek, but she might as well be talking to the wall when she goes to him for help. He always says that he is going to take care of it and nothing happens as usual. In the past, the kids would never put anything in writing about the illegal restraints by staff for fear of retaliation by the vengeful staff. It was always the staff's word against the kid's word and the staff always won...

The kids still continued to complain, but they don't expect anything to be done about it. The kids only casually talk about illegal restraints anymore because they know it's not a big deal at God's Love Institute. If the staff finds out that the kids made a complaint, they will immediately retaliate in some way against the kid. They might restrain the kid more often, they might restrict food that he/she is supposed to get, and they might not even let the kid get any phone calls from home. The staff already treats them bad, but the treatment will get increasingly worse. Maybe Miss Linda and I can get something done to get to finally break up the Three Stooges...

Miss Linda and I had a private meeting with Mr. Derek to give him the information about the restraint of Jonah. We told him that we had a witness who was willing to testify verbally and in writing about what he saw Mr. Larry and Mr. Moe do to Jonah. Mr. Derek said, "I'll investigate and get back to you as soon as I can. If there was some wrong-doing, I'll take care of it". I asked him would he let us know about his results soon and he said yes. Miss Linda and I stared at each other briefly and quietly walked out of his office. We both knew that this asshole was going to cover this up just like all the other abuse cases. We could tell by his demeanor and the way he couldn't look us in the eyes when he talked to us. I figured since we told him that we had something in writing about the restraint, he might be encouraged to really do something. I hope that I am finally right this time...

Several weeks later and there still was no word on what happened to Jonah. I talked to Jonah several times and his only comment was, "Ain't anything going to happen to them so I got nothing to say. You know how it is here; they always get away with this shit". All I could do was just walk away because he is absolutely right, sorry to say. I finally saw Mr. Derek walking down the sidewalk outside of the units one day. He told me that he checked everything out and there was nothing done wrong by the staff members. I didn't say anything because I was just amazed that he was able to get away with such blatant and obvious abuse of these poor children. As I was walking away, he said sarcastically, "You going to be alright with this?" I angrily said, "If that's the way it is, then that's the way it is. I'll talk to you later"...

I believe the only reason he is covering for these stooges is because he doesn't want to do the paperwork or hire new people to take their place. If the paperwork is the problem, I'll do the paperwork for him. If he wants, I will even hire some people to take their place. Maybe I should let him know what I'm willing to do to get rid of the stooges in this unit. This will be some more ignorance to write in my notes about this ungodly place... **"Believe in Change"**

Chapter 12

"Who's your Baby's Daddy?"

My wife told me that one of the girls is unfortunately pregnant. She said the girl's name is Ezra, a 12 year old African American in her unit. She said that the girl is two months pregnant and the company doesn't know what to do about it. This company doesn't condone abortions because of its Catholic background. They don't want this information to get out to the public about a 12 year old getting pregnant while in their custody. God's Love Institute really doesn't want that kind of publicity because that would tarnish their name. God forbid the newspapers find out about this pregnancy that occurred under the supervision of God's Love Institute. Ezra doesn't go on any home visits, so she must have gotten pregnant by one of the boys on campus. I'm really not sure if the company can rule out the male staff completely. Maybe one of the staff raped this poor young girl; I certainly hope that's not the case. When the girl was questioned by female staff, she wouldn't say how or when she got pregnant. The only reason the staff found out was because of an annual blood test that all the kids have to take...

The boys have been known to sneak into the girls units at night because they knew that a few of the staff slept all night. The boys just had to crawl through a window that the girls left open for them and get in their beds to do whatever they wanted to. The boys could spend the whole night with a girl and go back to their unit in the morning before the staff wake up. It's my understanding that this activity has been going on for many years. Every once in a while, a staff would surprisingly wake up and catch a boy on top of a girl having sex. The staff would never write the incident up because the staff would get in trouble for sleeping on the job. They would simply walk the boy back to his unit and threaten to fuck him up if he mentioned this incident to anyone. They would also threaten the girl to keep her quiet; they would let her know that they would take away all of her privileges. I guess for the children, there are some rewards in working with staff that don't give a damn and who can't keep their eyes open. They can sneak out their rooms and have sex anytime they want to and that's got to be a good feeling for the children. I guess that's really stretching it to find something positive to say about the staff at this company...

The company keeps everything quiet about the pregnancy because they just weren't sure what to do. Ezra wanted to have the baby because she thought it would be exciting to have a child. Ezra is in the custody of the state; she has no family involved in her young confused life right now. She had no one to even tell about the pregnancy other than the staff at this company. The only one who gives a damn is my wife Janet and a few other caring staff. The company is concerned about what to do about the baby and no one seems to be concerned about what kind of effect it's going to have on Ezra...

In the not so distant past when the company thought a girl might be pregnant, they would sneak a (Day-after-pill) into the girl's food or in with her daily medication so she would have an abortion from the pill. This has been a well kept secret that usually stayed with the nurse and the staff. I wonder how many other secrets I'm going to find out about before I leave this company. I'll just continue to take notes; maybe this will make a good book someday...

My wife told me that the supervisor of the girls units Miss Ronda told all the staff at the team meeting about Ezra being pregnant. None of the staff seemed shocked about it; I guess they are used to hearing that kind of news. Miss Ronda didn't elaborate on what the company was planning to do about Ezra's situation. She just said, "Make sure that the night staff do bed checks every 15 minutes. We want to make sure no more boys are in the girl's rooms". She never mentioned anything about what to do if Ezra needed to be restrained, considering that she is pregnant...

I guess she wasn't concerned with a young 12 year old getting physically restrained while she is two months pregnant. Maybe she is hoping that there is a restraint and Ezra will somehow conveniently lose the baby. The staff didn't ask what to do if they had to restrain Ezra; I guess they aren't concerned either. Janet asked her about restraining Ezra because she was very concerned that a restraint the wrong way could cause Ezra to lose the baby. Miss Ronda's response was, "Business as usual, we got to do what we got to do in order to maintain complete control of our units...

A week later, Janet came to work on a Saturday morning (7:00am) to begin her weekend shift (7am – 11pm). Upon doing her bed checks, she noticed that Ezra was gone so she asked Miss Kathy about it and she smugly said, "That little ungrateful bitch was acting up and we had to restrain her little ass. We fucked her up bad; me and Miss Sandra put a hurting on her this time. Unfortunately we had to take her to the hospital because she kept complaining about her side hurting. Now the doctor says that she has a broken rib and she lost that damn illegitimate baby. She didn't need a damn baby anyway". Before Janet could say anything to Miss Kathy, she quickly turned and hurried down the stairs to go home. Janet couldn't understand why Miss Kathy was so cold and heartless about the entire situation with Ezra...

Later on that day, Janet took a few girls (3) from the unit to the hospital to see how Ezra was doing. While they were driving to the hospital the girls told Janet the whole story about what happened to Ezra. Esther did most of the talking and she said, "Miss Ronda was sitting down at the dining room table constantly questioning Ezra about her being pregnant. She wanted to know where she had sex at and who the boy she was with. Miss Ronda told Ezra that she would be on room restriction until she got that information she wanted. Ezra got angry and said that she wanted to talk to her Case Manager. She grabbed the phone and quickly started dialing a few numbers, but was interrupted before she could complete the phone number...

Miss Ronda told her in a loud angry voice to put the phone down and started slowly walking towards Ezra. She took the phone and violently busted Miss Ronda in the side of her head as she reached her hand out to get the phone. Miss Ronda fell to the floor instantly holding her head in pain. Ezra was getting ready to hit her again when Miss Ronda tactfully kicked her in the stomach. Ezra went down to the floor instantly screaming in pain, saying loudly, "My baby, oh my baby". Before she could get another word out of her mouth, Miss Kathy and Miss Sandra started repeatedly punching her in the face. When Miss Ronda saw the staff attacking Ezra, she quietly left the room and went into the bathroom...

Maybe she was addressing her injuries or maybe she wanted to give the staff some room so they could really work Ezra over without there being any supervisor around. Ezra attempted to fight back, but she was just outnumbered and outweighed by the two grown people beating up on her. The more she tried to fight back, the more the staff beat on her. They mercilessly beat her for about 15 minutes until they saw blood coming from between Ezra's legs. There was a lot of blood flowing onto the floor and that's the only reason they stopped. Miss Ronda came out of the bathroom and told them to put her in the van and take her to the hospital. Miss Janet, you could probably see the trail of blood going up the side walk to where the van was parked today". Miss Janet was simply amazed to hear the story that was coming out of the girl's mouth...

When they arrived at the hospital everyone was amazed to see all the cuts and bruises on Ezra's face, neck and arms. Tears came to Janet's eyes instantly and then all the girls started crying. The shield of toughness that all these girls surround their lives with has apparently been compromised after looking at Ezra. Normally, if you see any of these girls crying it is because they are angry, but in this case they seem to be crying because they are sad about another individual. In many ways this is a breakthrough for them because it has taken many years of disappointment and hatred to become the way they are. They are letting out emotions that they never thought they had inside of them and this is a good thing. Maybe now they will allow themselves to feel sadness again and not worry so much about looking or being tough…

Janet sat next to Ezra and held her hand gently to console her. Janet squeezed her hand tightly and she asked her how she felt. Ezra started crying and angrily said, "They killed my baby Miss Janet, them dirty bitches killed my baby". Janet wasn't sure what to say in response to Ezra's comment, so she just listened a little more and let her vent. Ezra went on to say, "Miss Ronda kicked me in my stomach on purpose because that old white bitch didn't want me to have a baby. She's a murderer and no ones going to do a damn thing about it. It just ain't fair; I'm going to kill that white ass bitch when I get back to the unit. I should have stabbed her in the head instead of hitting her with the phone; that white bitch should be dead". Janet told Ezra that everything was going to be okay, just relax and get better. Before she left, (an hour later) she told Ezra that if she felt that she was mistreated she should let her Case Manager know and anyone else that will listen to her…

The ride back to the unit was a quiet and long one. Miss Janet broke the silence by saying, "How do you girls feel about what happened to Ezra?" There was a momentary silence and then they all started talking at the same time. Anger filled the air as each girl vented loudly and from the heart. Janet knew that if the girls didn't get to verbally let off steam before they got to the unit; it would come out in a physically negative way. When they pulled into the parking space at the unit 45 minutes later, all the girls thanked Miss Janet for taking them to the hospital. They also thanked her for letting them talk about what happened to Ezra. The girls told Miss Janet that since they got to talk about the incident; they feel a little better now…

This whole ordeal was very traumatic for Janet because she is very sensitive when it comes to the staff mistreating children. She and I talked about her quitting shortly afterwards, but I talked her out of it. I told her that if she quits, then who will the girls have to watch over them? She smiled and said, "I guess your right when I think about it like that. They do need you and me, who else are going to be there for them". I told her that the children are the only reason I'm still working at this ungodly place. God has chosen this path for us, who are we to go up against God. This has become even more personal to me now, after seeing my wife so upset. I don't have all the answers yet, but through prayer I know God will give them to me...
"Believe in Change"

Chapter 13

"The Bug- A- Boo's"

a few months later Janet gets a job working on the night shift so that we can hopefully spend more quality time together. Her new supervisor's name is Miss Cathy. On Janet's unit named "St. Monica" an all-girls unit, all the staff and kids began to have continuous problems with bug bites. When she went to work at night 11 p.m. to 7 a.m. she came home with numerous bug bites on her arms and legs. She thinks that she is getting chewed up by mosquitoes in the units and it's no big deal. So every night before she goes to work she sprays her body with bug repellent and expects it to work against the bug bites. No one has seen any of the mosquitoes yet, but they are pretty sure that is what's biting everyone…

The next time Janet had got bitten, she felt something slowly crawling up her neck. She began desperately ripping at her clothes trying to get to the spot where she felt the bug crawling. It took her a few minutes to find the bug, but she killed it by smashing it with her fingers. She decided to put it in a plastic bag to take home because she wanted to find out exactly what kind of insect was chewing on her. 30 minutes after her bite, her neck began rapidly swelling up. She contacted her supervisor right away and Miss Cathy asked her what she wants to do. Janet said in an irritated voice, "I need to get out of here right now; I am too upset to work tonight". Miss Cathy calmly said, "If you need to go home I certainly understand; I'll get someone to cover your shift so don't worry about that". So Janet went home at 2 a.m; she was very upset and irritated…

Janet went to see her personal doctor the next day because she wanted the incident documented and she needed some medication to take the swelling down from the bug bite. We looked on the internet that following morning and found out the bugs that have been biting everyone are called "Bedbugs", blood sucking little creatures that live off the blood of humans. Janet was pissed and infuriated, she notified Miss Cathy the same day by email. She wanted to make sure that she had some form of documentation about the whole incident. That is why she chose to e-mail Miss Cathy. She reluctantly went back to work the next day, but she took a beach chair to sit in. She didn't want to sit on that bug infested furniture anymore…

Miss Cathy asked to get the bedbug from Janet so she could give it to the Maintenance Supervisor named Mr. Kent. Janet reluctantly gave her the bug because she thought that someone was going to really do something to get rid of them. Any company with just a little bit of sense would try to get rid of the bedbugs as soon as possible. It would be crazy not to do something about this right away because these creatures spread like the plague…

After Janet started sitting in her own personal chair she fortunately stopped getting bitten. Three weeks goes by and still nothing is done about the bedbugs in St. Monica. The kids and staff are still complaining about getting bitten, but no one is listening or they just don't give a damn. One of the kids named Zephaniah got bit so badly one night that the staff had to take her to see the nurse that next morning. The nurse named Miss Susan told Zephaniah that the bites were from spiders. The staff found out that Nurse Susan was directed by the (Director of Residential Living); Miss Lisa to say all bites was done by spiders…

Nurse Susan actually told one kid that the bites were psychological and they would go away if she quit thinking about them. This nurse didn't go to school for psychology, but yet she was able to determine that the bites on this child are more than likely psychological. What a bunch of bullshit! They had the poor child thinking that her mind was making the bug bites appear all over her body. This particular young girl had 55 bites all over her body in various areas. It is amazing what this company is trying to do to save some money…

One day Janet forgot to bring her chair to work and she has to use one of the unit's chairs again. About half way through the shift unfortunately she got bit again in spite of having her body covered by clothing from her feet all the way up to the neck area. A bedbug still got into her clothing and started insatiably chewing on her. She instantly ran down to the bathroom to take her clothes off to get the bedbug out. Janet was frantically ripping at her clothes trying to get them off. It was as if each article of clothing was burning her flesh. Finally, she found the bug conveniently hiding inside the lower part of her blouse. The bug was still alive and looking for more blood to suck. She quickly threw it on the floor and frantically smashed it with her shoe…

Sweat was coming off her forehead as she continued to look through her clothing for more bugs. After 15 minutes of meticulously going through every stitch of clothing, she was satisfied that it was safe to put her clothes back on. She sat down on the bathroom floor holding her head and thinking about how crazy this is to have to go through something like this at her workplace. Why should anyone have to come to work and worry about getting chewed up by a bedbugs…

Janet came out of the bathroom really pissed off and calls the supervisor on the phone. Miss Cathy said she would be right over to talk to her. Ten minutes later they are in the office downstairs talking. Miss Cathy calmly says with a concerned look on her face, "I'm sorry you got bit again, Mr. Kent is going to take all of the furniture out tomorrow and spray the building. We are going to have all the kids sleep in the main office building overnight until the unit airs out. Until then you can take the rest of the day off. How's that sound to you?" Janet bit her tongue to stop her from cursing Miss Cathy out and just said calmly, "Okay". She knew that everything her supervisor said was a bunch of bullshit. Janet wondered how people like her slept at night…

Now when Janet is at home she is constantly wiping anything off her and my clothing that resembles a bug. She checks the bed before she lies down and all the furniture before she sits on it. She is beginning to drive me crazy with her paranoid behavior. I wasn't sure if she didn't need to go and talk to a psychologist. I told her to contact the "Department of Welfare" (DPW) to see what they could do about the bedbugs at God's Love Institute...

She did and they told her that they were going to do a thorough investigation as soon as possible. They also wanted to know if she could bring them a few of the bugs to their office. By this time, all the staff has a few dead bugs hidden in plastic bags in the trunks of their cars for evidence. She also took some bugs to the "Department of Health" (D.O.H.) and dropped them off. She requested to stay anonymous in both cases because she didn't want to get fired from her job for opening her mouth...

That following week Mr. Kent moved all the hallway furniture out of the building to have a clean and sanded. The kids have to sleep at the main building in the conference room on the floor for one night while Mr. Kent supposedly sprayed the bedrooms. For some reason he only did the upstairs and not the whole building. I guess he only did the upstairs because the company wanted to save money...

He didn't spray the building for bedbugs; he sprayed for everything but bedbugs. I don't know what he was thinking because what he did will not get rid of the bedbugs. I guess this cheap ass company doesn't want to hire a professional exterminator to do the job correctly. Janet found cans of spray bombs named, "Sano Guard total release fogger" in the garbage can outside of the girls units. She took an empty can of it home with her to keep as evidence to show that the building wasn't sprayed for bedbugs. They did put different furniture in the hallway for the staff to sit on until the other furniture is done...

For two weeks no one got bit and it was looking like the bedbugs were finally taken care of. First the kids started getting attacked again and than the staff also started noticing bites on them. Miss Cathy heard about the bedbugs being back and let Janet work in another unit because she didn't want to hear her complain anymore. That made Janet very happy to get out of that unit. Mr. Kent was calling anyone who was complaining a "bugaboo". I guess he somehow managed to find some humor in hearing about the staff getting bitten by bedbugs. None of the staff agreed with that dumb ass humor of his. I guess it's easy to have a sense of humor if you are not the one getting chewed on by bedbugs...

I don't know why (D.P.W.) or the Health Department hasn't done anything to make God's Love Institute do something about this sad situation. Does anyone give a damn about this sad situation? Does anyone give a damn about these kids? The company certainly makes enough money to hire an exterminator so why don't they. I understand why the company hasn't done anything, they just don't care. Why hasn't the state done something to help these children? All these questions and not one single answer...

It has been two months and finally God's Love Institute hires a professionally to exterminate the unit. I believe (DPW) made them do something because they sure weren't going to do anything on their own. I even contacted the news stations, but none of them came out to investigate. I guess children getting bit by bedbugs isn't news worthy. If one of the kids gets bit and dies, maybe that will get the attention of someone. This is really a sad state-of-affairs when it is okay for a multi-million dollar company allows the children to sleep with bedbugs. What has this country come to? A lot of the children who stay in the residential living never had bedbugs at their personal homes and they didn't make millions of dollars. This company gets paid too much money to let something like this happen and not do anything about it right away... **"Believe in Change"**

Chapter 14

"They are back"

One night when Janet got to work at St. Monica, she noticed that 8 out of the 10 girls in the unit were sleeping in a doorway of their rooms. State law stipulates that all children must sleep in beds and not on floors based on DPW regulations. Janet asked Miss Gadget why are girls on the floor? Miss Gadget said, "I already called Miss Cathy and she said leave them there because them god damned bedbugs are back again. She told me that the girls refused to sleep in their beds until something is done about the bugs". Janet sympathetically said, "I can't blame these poor kids for not wanting to sleep with bedbugs crawling all over their body. As long as the supervisor knows then we are covered"…

Janet has been working with Miss Gadget for a few months steady at St. Monica. Janet has found that she is a very meticulous lady and everything has to be in place in order for her to be comfortable at the job. At first, it was hard for Janet to work with Miss Gadget because she was so picky about where everything needed to be. She has been working at God's Love Institute for five years on the night shift at the same unit. She is a white female in her late 50s who appears to be just another staff who works here just for money. Miss Gadget sleeps the whole night and even the bedbugs can't keep her awake. She sleeps all night because she needs the rest for her other job as a waitress. Janet is always amazed how comfortable she is about sleeping while never knowing if a child is going to come out of their room and cut her throat. Janet never sleeps at work, but that doesn't mean she doesn't get tired and feel like closing her eyes for a little while...

Janet has found out that the best time to talk to Miss Gadget is the first hour of work. She is usually only awake for the first hour of every shift anyway. She talks enough in the first hour to last all night long. Janet listens patiently as she talks about the bugs in the unit again. Miss Gadget said enthusiastically, "The bedbug jumped down from the light fixture into Mr. Tony's shirt and it started biting him on his back. The other staff saw the bug jump down on him as he walked down the upstairs hall. At first she thought it was a piece of dirt that fell from the filthy light fixture so she didn't get alarmed. Mr. Tony frantically began trying to scratch his back, but because he is seriously fat there was no way he was going to reach his back with his short fat arms. He began rubbing his back against the wall trying to ease the pain of being constantly bitten. After that didn't work, he laid on the floor and was rolling around like a fat dog with fleas or ticks. This comedy show went on for almost 10 minutes until the other staff decided to help him find the elusive bedbug...

One by one all the kids were standing in a doorway watching Mr. Tony lying on the floor looking like a beached whale with fleas. The kids were laughing loudly until they saw what Miss Juanita bravely and courageously pulled off Mr. Tony's massive back. When she saw what was on his back, she took the tweezers out the first aid kit that was at the desk. She nervously pulled the bug off his back and put it in a clear sandwich bag for further observation. Now all the girls are screaming in fear because they know that the dreaded bedbugs are back looking for blood again. Mr. Tony had 10 bites on his back, this bug was really hungry. Miss Juanita showed the bug to Mr. Tony so he could also confirm that it was a bedbug. Frustrated, He said "I thought they killed all those little motherfuckers. Did they exterminate this building or not?" Miss Juanita said, "It looks like Mr. Kent lied about exterminating this building; what other explanation could there be"...

The girls all said at almost the same time, "I'm not sleeping in these beds anymore. We shouldn't have to sleep with the bugs on us". Miss Gadget told Janet, "That is why the girls aren't in their beds tonight". Janet said, "Does Mr. Kent know about the bugs being back yet". Miss Gadget says (sounding very sleepy now), "Miss Cathy said he knows and he is going to take care of it again". Janet said angrily, "He couldn't have done it right the first time. I thought we were done with this mess". Miss Gadget quietly said, "Well I guess Mr. Kent did it the God's Love Institute way, which is usually the wrong way or the cheapest way". Janet said, "Well I'm not going to continue to worry about bugs so he better do something fast". By the time Janet finished unfolding her lawn chair to sit down, Miss Gadget was snoring loudly. Not even the return of bedbugs is going to stop her from getting paid to sleep by this company...

Its a few weeks later and still nothing have been done about the bedbugs. The bugs have now spread to other units because the staff doesn't always work in the same units. The bugs can easily be transported on the clothing of the staff and that's what I believe is happening. Some staff is complaining to each other about finding bugs in their houses and cars. The staff doesn't dare complain to management for fear of losing their jobs. Janet has a ritual that she performs every day before leaving the job. She checks her clothing religiously to determine if any bugs are trying to get a ride home with her. Almost all the staff has got in the habit of checking all their personal items for bedbugs. None of the staff are sure if they can get reimbursed if they need to hire an exterminator for their homes. It is bad enough that staff have to work in an environment where there are bedbugs, now they have to worry about taking the bugs from this job into their personal lives. These stressful working conditions are taking a toll on the staff and the children...

It is already difficult to work with troubled youth because the staff never knows how the child's going to be acting each day. Now the staff has to contend with the children and the bedbugs each time they come to work. Restraints have probably doubled since the arrival of the bugs six months ago. The lasting effects of emotionally dealing with this insane work environment might be measured in years. I doubt if there is anything the company could do to ever make the staff or children think that they give a damn about them. The staff understands that it's the company that made a decision not to do anything about the bugs, but the kids blame everything on the staff. This is added tension between the staff and the children...

In spite of the numerous phone calls to the DPW, no one has determined that the situation warrants coming to the campus to investigate. Janet came to work one night and she had to work with a female staff named Miss Donna for the first time. She is a 22-year-old white female who has only been working for a company for four months. The story on her is that she is waiting to hear back from the police academy about employment. She is very outspoken; she doesn't mind telling you exactly what's on her mind. She is only about 5 feet tall and weighs about 100 pounds soaking wet. Most of the kids are bigger than her, but she is very feisty and don't take any shit from the kids...

15 minutes into this shift, Janet noticed her crawling on the floor with plastic gloves and thick goggles on her eyes. Janet's first thought was that she was hurt or crazy. Janet curiously said, "Are you okay, do you need some help?" Miss Donna smiled and said, no thanks, I'm just collecting bugs in this clear freezer bag. I collect bugs every night and I put them in the furniture at the fucking Main building. So if you go in the Main building don't sit in any of the chairs over there. Janet quietly said, "How long have you been doing that?" Miss Donna said with a serious look on her face, "For about two weeks". I thought that I would share the bugs with the assholes over there since we have so many of them crawling around over here"...

When Janet heard this comment, a feeling of enjoyment passed through her entire body. Janet had joyous visions of the Sister running up and down the hallways in the main building begging people to help her get the bugs off of her. This vision brought a big smile to Janet's face. This is a smile that she hasn't had in a long time. She asked Miss Donna if she wanted any of the other bugs that the staff finds on their shift. Miss Donna said, "The more the merrier, I just want to make the people in the Main building just as happy as we are over here"...

It didn't take long before the big shots in the Main building were getting chewed up by the bedbugs that Miss Donna so kindly deposited at predetermined areas throughout the building. She found great pleasure in sliding several of the biggest bugs underneath the Sister's door to her office. After several days of the Sister getting attacked by bedbugs she called the (Director of Maintenance) Mr. Kent to exterminate her office. He didn't tell the Sister that he found bedbugs because she thought that they were exterminated from campus already. He embellished a little and told her that someone must have carelessly brought fleas from home into the building. He said that he would have the whole building exterminated on the weekend when there is no one in the building...

Bedbugs, which can be difficult to spot, are becoming even tougher to eradicate as they spread and their resistance to some pesticides grow. In response, pest control companies are adopting new tactics. Some companies are using a technology that sprays the bugs with an icy carbon dioxide to kill them. In some cases they use a device similar to a giant hairdryer to heat up a room and bake the bugs to death. There are companies who will remove people's furniture from their homes and fumigate with a poisonous gas. Believe it or not there is a method that uses specially trained dogs to track down tiny bedbugs and their eggs, helping exterminators target spraying. At one university they are studying bedbugs' behavior and attempt to develop a trap that simulates a typical victim such as a sleeping human...

Professional treatments, including many of the conventional method still being used, can start at about several hundred dollars and reach into the thousands. In the Hopesville area, the fight against bedbugs is picking up. Pest control experts say reports of infestations continue to be on the upswing in this area. In Hopesville, bedbug calls has gone up 20 to 30% between 2006 and 2007. A simple solution to get rid of the common bedbug has proven elusive since the brown, wingless creature made resurgence in the United States about five years ago. Both Entomologist and the Pest control industry say they have seen a rise in the infestation of homes and hotels. Bedbugs are slightly smaller than the apple seed and hide in the folds and seams of mattresses and other furniture, emerging at night to feed on the warm-blooded host, which in this case are the children or the staff. Part of what makes bedbugs so tricky to eradicate is that the insects are not confined to the beds...

They live in drapes, behind wall hangers, and cracks in the wall plaster, and even in light fixtures and electronics. Further complicating matters, a female bedbug can deposit their tiny eggs around the room. The bugs are transported from one location to another in luggage or clothing. Bedbug bites can produce itchy welts, but the bugs are not known to carry any diseases. Still they can be quite a nuisance and take a powerful psychological toll...

Some staff and kids haven't sleep well for months, worrying that every itch is a bug on them. That following weekend Mr. Kent had the building professionally exterminated for bedbugs, but paid extra money to have the contract read that it was exterminated for fleas to cover his ass. This is what the exterminator did for Mr. Kent, all the furniture in the building was washed with very hot water that was at least 120 plus degrees. The exterminator used a special vacuum tool to remove bedbugs from hiding places such as chairs, couches, floor cracks, under carpets and etc. the exterminator explained to Mr. Kent that he could not guarantee that the bugs will not come back. Hopefully Mr. Kent will get it in his head that there is no easy way out when dealing with these bedbugs. It simply can't continue to be all about the money anymore...

"Believe in Change"

Chapter 15

"Sharing the Bugs"

Everyone on campus quickly heard about the bugs at the Main building. This was the first time that the staff and the kids had something to smile about in a long time. Throughout the whole campus all the staff and all the kids were laughing and joking about the bedbugs being in the Main building. The smiles of joy soon turned to frowns when they heard about how quick the Main building was exterminated. Hearing that news was like a vicious slap in the face to the staff because of how fast the company reacted to having bedbugs in the Main building. There wasn't even any consideration given to exterminating any of the other units on campus yet. A week later Miss Donna diligently started putting bugs back in the main building again. Now she has the support of all the staff on campus...

All of the staff is gathering bugs for Miss Donna; she is like a "queen-bee" and the other staff are the "worker-bees" going out and collecting bugs for her. This is the first time that I have seen everyone come together and support the same issue. Hopefully this will be the beginning of all the staff working together as a team. The staff was more concerned about catching bugs than they were worried about the bugs biting them. Maybe this could be the beginning of a new era for the staff at God's Love Institute. Maybe they will finally quit taking shit from this company, time will tell...

On many occasions Miss Donna had as many as 50 bugs in her bag to put in the Main building. She is very serious about planting the bugs in the building. On the nights that she was going to sneak into the building she wore a camouflage military uniform. She has spent two years in the Army and kept some of her uniforms when she got discharged three years ago. She put the vast majority of the hungry bugs in Mr. Kent's office since he is the main person who decides whether or not to have a real exterminator come and do the units...

The next day after Miss Donna put the bedbugs in Mr. Kent's office and he became the main source of blood for the hungry little creatures. For two hours straight the bedbugs viciously chewed on him before he realized what was happening. While he was sitting in his big soft leather chair making useless attempts at scratching his back and his legs; he saw a bedbug crawling out of the phone. He panics as he frantically stumbled out of his office into the hallway. As he was standing in the hallway desperately wiping his clothes as if they were on fire, out the corner of his eye he saw the Sister curiously staring at him. Before he could say anything the Sister smiled and said, "Are you okay Mr. Kent? Is there something on your clothing that you are trying to get? Did you get some dust on you? You look like you are being attacked by some bumblebees". He said, "I am all right; I was just trying to get a spider web off of me. Thanks for asking, I have to get back to work now". Without waiting for a response from her, he rushes back into his office and stands in the corner surveying the room. He is thinking to himself, what in the hell is going on? Why are there still bedbugs in this damn building? Is someone playing games with me? I have to figure out what's going on and I have to do it fast...

Now Mr. Kent has to worry about losing his job because if the Sister gets bit one more time by a bedbug she is definitely going to terminate him. Before he leaves his office he carefully checks his clothing to ensure that there are no bugs on them. His only hope is that the bugs are isolated just in his office for now. If they are just in his office, he will be able to get rid of them real fast and without suspicion...

After he was sure that there were no bugs on him, he then locked his office up tightly and walked down to the Sister's office. He wanted to make sure that no bugs had returned to her office. Mr. Kent stuck his head in her doorway and said, "Good morning sister, I was just checking to see if you're having any problems with them filthy bugs anymore". She smiled and said, "Thank God they're gone and I can relax now. Thank you for getting rid of them so quickly and promptly. I always know that I can count on you when I need you. If I have any additional problems you will be the first to know"...

That was good news for Mr. Kent and now he still has to figure out what his next move is going to be about these damn bedbugs. He could actually go out and exterminate the bugs from the units on campus, but that would cost a lot of money. The money that was allocated the first time to exterminate the bedbugs he used for something else. In Mr. Kent's contract there is a paragraph stating that all the money he helped the company save in maintenance fees; a certain percentage would go towards his salary. Rumor is that at least 30% of that will be added to his salary this year. Now it makes more sense why he is being very tight with how much money he spends on maintenance of the units. Sooner or later the issue with the bedbugs is going to come back and haunt him...

No matter what Mr. Kent did, he could not get rid of the bedbugs in the main building because Miss Donna made sure that she put new bedbugs in the building every chance she got. No matter how hard he has been trying to save money, he is simply going to have to spend some money to get rid of these bedbugs on campus. He is putting his master plan together to do one unit every week until all the units on campus are done. Obviously there is not going to be any bonus money in his salary this year because he is about to spend it all on them damn bedbugs. He actually has the nerve to look at it as if he is really spending money out of his pocket. What kind of man would put money over to welfare of these poor children? What kind of company would hire a man like that? It is just amazing what some people will do for the love of money...

Once Mr. Kent began exterminating the units, then Miss Donna stopped taking bedbugs to the main building. She has promised all the staff that if he doesn't continue to get rid of the bedbugs that she will start putting the bugs back in the Main building again. I am sure that if the Sister has a problem with bugs one more time, there is a good chance Mr. Kent will be looking for another job. I hope that this is the last that I have to write about kids getting bitten by bedbugs at God's Love Institute. Of course this won't be the first time that I thought the bugs were gone... **"Believe in Change"**

Chapter 16

"The Plan of the Three Stooges"

$\mathcal{I}$'m having problems getting Mr. Derek to give me the kid's allowance money and the unit's activity money in a timely manner. Each kid is supposed to get three dollars a week and the whole unit gets $100 a month for activities. Right now, unfortunately I'm already two months behind in money that I owe the kids. I've been using my hard earned personal money so the kids can get their allowances on time. There hasn't been any money for activities so the children haven't been doing anything off campus. Not being able to get this money on time has really been frustrating for me. Mr. Derek is lazy and never does anything on time. It is time for this foolishness to end and I'm going to tell him that I don't want this supervisor's job anymore. I haven't been able to do anything to help the children and I really believe that he is stealing the kid's money. The money is not coming to the unit so where is it going. Where is the kid's money? Where is the unit's money? There are so many unanswered questions about one man so I need to get out of this supervisory position before I get blamed for this stolen money...

Mr. Derek called me at home and said that he needed to talk to me about something very important. I wasn't sure what he wanted, but at least I could tell him that I no longer wanted to be supervisor of St. Pauls. The next day he met me at the unit and we walked over to his office to talk in private. He started by saying in a serious voice, "Do you want to be supervisor at St. Pauls?" I was surprised to hear that because I wasn't sure why he asked that particular question. I had to think fast so I told him calmly, "I don't mind being supervisor, but I need to be able to make some changes in the way the unit is run". He said without looking at me, "All that will come in time, but for now we need to talk about some other issues concerning the staff and you at the unit". Now I really didn't have any idea what he was talking about and where he was going with this conversation...

Mr. Derek said, "The staff has been saying that you have been leaving work early, at least a couple hours. They also have been saying that you go to the gym everyday for three hours at a time without taking any kids with you. They say that you leave the unit for hours at a time and no one knows where you are at; they can't contact you. Is there any truth to any of these allegations?" I told him, "No, anyone that knows me wouldn't even consider any truth to these outrageous accusations"...

He didn't mention any names, but I knew it was Curly, Moe, and Larry (the three stooges). They have been doing everything to undermine my authority at the unit since I have become supervisor. They would leave me upstairs for hours without giving me a break and when I would call downstairs no one would answer the phone. They would change the daily logs that I wrote in by taking my name out and putting their names in. There were a few times when someone let the air out of my tires at work. My lunch would be gone or there would be some food missing from it. I believe that Mr. Curly was stealing my food; he has been stealing the kid's food for years...

I personally have seen Mr. Curly loading up the trunk of his car on numerous occasions at the end of the shift, with trays of the children's food. He has been stealing the kid's Christmas gifts for many years and I'm not sure what he does with them. He calls himself a "Church Deacon"; I call him an "Abusive Demon" who was sent by the Devil to torment God's children. He is always complaining that he is underpaid, but for a person with only a high school diploma or less, he really shouldn't even be working with "at risk-youth". I really believe that he is a functional illiterate and has been getting away with it for years.

I'm positive that this man and the many other staff that work here will burn in hell some day for what they have done to these children...

I guess if this company adds up all the food and kid's donations that the staff has stolen, they would probably be getting paid $20 dollars an hour. Maybe the company knows that these staff steal from the kids and just look the other way because it's cheaper than paying them more money. This company certainly has been getting enough complaints from the kids about food and gifts disappearing mysteriously...

Mr. Derek told me that I needed to figure out a way to get the staff and myself on the same page. He said, "I'll set up a team meeting with just you and the other staff. This way everyone can air out their problems and we can move forward". I said reluctantly, "If you think a meeting will help then I'm willing to try it"...

We had the meeting that next week in the unit's television room. Only one person showed up and that was Mr. Jackson, who I didn't have any problems with anyway. I knew that Larry, Curly and Moe weren't going to be there because they are the ones who are trying to get me fired. They are all cowards in my opinion because they were scared to show up and face me man to man. I'm not going to mention anything to Mr. Derek about me wanting to abdicate myself from the position of supervisor right now. I don't want the staff to think they had something to do with my decision to quit this position. I will never give the Three Stooges the satisfaction of thinking that their plan to get me fired worked...

I was very disappointed and hurt that Mr. Derek actually asked me about the allegations (lies) of the staff. If he would have taken time to get to know me, he would know that I wouldn't do any of the things the staff told him. He should be backing me up instead of teaming up with the three stooges. This leads me to believe that he is looking for a reason to get me out of this supervisor position. I have always had the feeling that he was the one who was trying to stop me from getting the supervisory job in the first place. He probably wanted a supervisor who he can control and manipulate and found out that I am not one. He can't do that with me, I'm too smart, plus I actually give a damn what happens to the kids. I decided to just lay back and reevaluate my situation as a supervisor. I knew that I wouldn't be able to make any positive changes while I worked for Mr. Derek so my plan was still to step down from the supervising position...

A few months later I happily told Mr. Derek that I no longer wanted the job and I wanted to go back to my Primary Youth Counselor position. He told me that I would have to wait awhile until he found someone else to take the job. I didn't want to, but I agreed to it anyways because I was happy just to know that I was going to be stepping down. I doubt if anyone else would take this job because no one really wants to work for an idiot like Mr. Derek. The only chance of getting this position filled would be to hire someone from the outside who doesn't know about Mr Derek and the staff that work at St. Pauls. All the staff thought I was crazy for taking the supervisor's job when it first came open. Now I definitely see why they thought I was crazy for taking the job. At least I found out what kind of help these children need in residential living and it's a lot...

One day Mr. Larry and a staff named Mr. Tony who is from another unit (St. Johns), was arguing about this white female staff named Amy. She is not very attractive, but there must be something about her that these two idiots enjoy and think she is worth fighting about. The rumor is that she spends money on both of them and they are using her for all the free gifts that they are getting. I'm sure she is getting something in return for all the gifts; my only guess is that it has to be sex. Of course Mr. Larry and Mr. Tony aren't the greatest looking guys in the world either so I guess it all evens out...

Mr. Larry and Mr. Tony were in the hallway of St. Pauls where all the kids could hear them arguing. Mr. Tony is an African American man, weighing about 450 pounds on a 5"10' frame. He is fat and happy and apparently doesn't care what anyone else thinks about how he looks. As far as I know he has never considered going on any type of a diet. He is in his early 30's, he wears thick black rimmed eye glasses and always has a smile on his face. He has long black dreadlock hair that exposes his now receding hairline. He and Mr. Larry are having an ongoing love Affair with Miss Amy and they both just found out about each other from the other staff...

Mr. Tony told Mr. Larry in a loud agitated voice, "You're married, so why are you messing with Amy anyway. You need to go home to your wife after work instead of sneaking around with Amy. She is my woman and that how it's going to be right now". Mr. Larry said in retaliation, "I don't know what you're talking about, me and Amy is just friends". Mr. Tony said sarcastically, "Amy told me that you guys just had sex the other day in the kitchen at St. Johns on top of the table. This is the same place where the kids eat their food and socialize. There are still cum stains on the table because neither one of you cleaned up your mess; she showed them to me you fucking asshole". Mr. Larry violently pushed Mr. Tony and said, "That bitch is lying, I'm a happily married man with small kids. What do I want with that fat ugly bitch?"

As he slowly walks away Mr. Tony firmly grabbed him from behind and they started wrestling until they both forcefully fell to the floor. I could almost feel the building shake like a small earthquake when they hit the floor. Now all the kids are standing in their doorway watching the action and excitement of two staff acting like fools. They rolled around on the floor in one big ball of arms and legs. I had no intentions of breaking the fight up; I wasn't going to get hurt trying to separate two grown men. They could kill each other and I wouldn't care; I am here for the kids not this foolishness. The kids seemed to be getting enjoyment from watching two grown men roll around on the floor. I figured the kids deserved some fun, since most of the time the staff didn't do anything with the kids to entertain them...

After ten minutes, Mr. Moe and Mr. Curly came running upstairs to see what was going on. They thought one of the kids was probably being restrained and they didn't want to miss out on the fun of joining in. They immediately broke the fight up as soon as they saw who it was. There were a few braids on the floor because Mr. Larry must have pulled some of Mr. Tony's hair out in the fight. Neither one of them knew how to fight; I've seen more action in girl fights in high school. It was like watching a black whale trying to make love to a seal on the beach. It wasn't a pretty thing to watch, but the kids seemed to enjoy it. I expected them to jump on each other again when they got up, but Mr. Tony just picked up his hair off the floor and went outside. He shouted from the bottom of the steps, "Only bitches pull hair when they fight". All the kids laughed loudly and so did I. I wish that I would have had time to make some popcorn for me and the kids, especially since there is never any unit money to take the kids to the movies...

"Believe in Change"

Chapter 17

"The Orgy that never Happened"

*T*wo months have passed since I asked to step down from the position of supervisor and Mr. Derek still can't find anyone to take this damn position. I talked to Mr. Derek again and told him that no matter what, I'm stepping down as the supervisor of this unit. He said, "I understand, but I need you to hang in there for two more weeks. After that you can go back to working your weekends again". I said, "Thank you" and quickly walked out of his office without saying goodbye. I'm sure he could tell by the tone of my voice that I had enough of his bullshit at St. Pauls. I really didn't believe that Mr. Derek was actively seeking a new supervisor. I didn't even hear of anyone being interviewed for the position. I know that no one on campus would take the job, but I'm sure he could have found someone from outside of the organization that would take the job. He talks a good game and that would be enough to get someone who doesn't know he's an asshole to agree to try the job out...

Two weeks later I started working the weekends again and I felt like a heavy weight had been lifted off my shoulders. Mr. Derek wasn't very happy with me stepping down from the position because now he really had to find a new supervisor. A (R.T.F.) unit has to have a supervisor or they will be out of compliance and the company could possibly lose some of their funding. This cheap ass company isn't going to lose any money if they can help it so I know they will hire someone very soon. I wasn't looking forward to working the weekends with Mr. Larry and his fat ass uncle Mr. Jerry. There is always some drama when those two are around each other. I don't like drama, but that is all that I have found working here. At least I won't have to work with Mr. Curly more than once a week; that is a blessing for me...

I don't feel that I was able to get anything done being a supervisor and that was disappointing for me. There were fewer restraints when I was supervisor and that's a good thing, but I was hoping to do so much more for the children. Everything else on the units is the same or worse. The kids still don't get their allowances on time and there is never any unit money for the kids to do things like movies, bowling and buying pizza. Some of the staff still dress like bums and seem happy about it. They are still overworked and underpaid; of course being underpaid is something that I didn't expect to change anyway. They still come to work late; I did want to change that...

What I found out is that the staff may come to work late, but they have one of the other staff swipe their timecards in as if they were on time. This has been going on for many years and this company had never considered checking to see if the staff is actually at work when they say they are. I imagine this company has lost millions because of the staff swiping the time clock for each other. A few of the staff may not make a lot of money, but they make up for it in what they steal from the company...

The kid named Ezekiel was turning 18 years old in a few days and he is getting ready to go live with his sister in Virginia. I only found out about it that Friday afternoon when I came to work. The other staff told me that he would be leaving Monday morning at 10:00am. My first weekend back was quiet considering that I had to work with Mr. Larry and his fat ass uncle Jerry. I got a phone call at home from Mr. Derek on Tuesday afternoon at 1:00pm. I was surprised to get a call from him because I wasn't the supervisor anymore. If I knew he was on the phone than I wouldn't have answered it. I really didn't want to deal with him no more than I had to. He said, "Hi Mr. Renaldo, Sorry for disturbing you at home, but this is pretty important". I'm thinking to myself, "What is he up to now? Who is telling lies on me now, which one of the three stooges is trying to get me fired now?" What kind of shit is about to come out of his mouth now?

Mr. Derek said, "How were things Sunday night before you left?" I told him, "Nice and quiet just the way I like it". After a short pause he said, "Something pretty serious happened after you left St. Pauls". I said curiously, "What happened". He said, "While the night staff was sleep, three of the boys were caught by the night supervisor Miss Cathy in Ezekiel's room. They were all taking turns having oral sex with each other. Miss Cathy caught them at 4:00 am when she came to give the night staff a 15 minute break"...

When she got to the unit, all the kids were up roaming the hallways doing whatever they wanted. Miss Cathy had come upstairs the back way, something she does sometimes if she is trying to catch a staff sleeping. The first person she saw was Jonah standing in his doorway; he was looking across the hall into Ezekiel's room. He saw Miss Cathy and pointed into Ezekiel's room with a smile on his face. She walked to the doorway of the room and her mouth dropped to the floor when she saw what was going on...

All four boys were lying in a circle on the floor and they were all naked from the waist down. The ages of the boys are from 14-18, with Ezekiel being the oldest. Their names are Nahum, Joel, Peter and Ezekiel. They were giving oral sex to each other. Miss Cathy stood there staring for several seconds, and then she ran down the hall to wake the staff up...

Normally there is supposed to be two staff members working, but the night shift was running short as usual so there was only one staff. The first thing Miss Cathy noticed about the staff that was asleep is that his penis was hanging out of his pants. This is a new staff named Mr. Troy; he has only been working for the company a few weeks. He is white male, in his late 40's, 5'10", and weighing 200 pounds. He has light brown hair, clean-shaved, wearing blue jeans and a white t-shirt. Miss

Cathy shouted loudly, "Fix your damn pants and bring your ass down here so you can help me get these boys back in their damn rooms"…

Mr. Troy fumbled with his pants trying to put his penis back inside. He staggered to his feet, barely awake and quickly followed her down the hall to Ezekiel's room. Miss Cathy turned the lights on and rushed in the room with Mr. Troy close behind her. Mr. Troy just stood there in shock as the boys scrambled to get their clothes back on. Miss Cathy said firmly, "Everyone go to their rooms right now". One by one, all the boys ran out the room, some were not even fully dressed yet. Ezekiel just sat on his bed calmly putting his clothes on as his room cleared out. Miss Cathy told Mr. Troy to make sure all the boys go to their own rooms. She told Ezekiel to come with her because she needed to know what happened. They went down to the unit's office to talk. She angrily said to Mr. Troy, "I'll be right back; you should have an Incident Report written by the time I get back"…

Miss Cathy asked Ezekiel to tell her how all the boys got into his room. He said, "Peter told Mr. Troy that he would suck his penis if he let them come to my room to say goodbye since this is going to be my last night here". She said, "So what you are saying is Mr. Troy agreed to let Peter give him oral sex so that the other boys could go into your room". Ezekiel said, "Yeah, Peter will do anything that I say because he says that he is in love with me. Mr. Troy turned all the hallway lights off and Peter started giving him oral sex while the other boys came to my room. Mr. Troy fell asleep after Peter was done, then he came down to celebrate with us"…

With a shocked look on her face Miss Cathy said, "Would you consider putting what you just said in writing?" He said, "Hell no, are you fucking crazy, I'm going home tomorrow and I will deny everything that happened tonight". She said angrily, "You know your 18 years old now and you could go to jail for having sex with minors". Ezekiel smiled and said, "You can't prove anything and I'll be home by the time you figure it all out. Besides, do you really want to tell people that your staff likes to get his penis sucked by teenage boys?" Miss Cathy said loudly, "Go to your room, I'll talk to you later"...

Miss Cathy went upstairs to talk to Mr. Troy again to hear his side of the story. He was still working on his Incident Report. She quietly sat down next to him, but didn't say anything for several minutes as she watched him finishing the incident report. Miss Cathy said, "Why was your penis hanging outside of your pants when I got here Mr. Troy?" He said, "I don't know, my zipper must have come loose and it fell out; I obviously don't wear underwear". She calmly said, "Did you talk to Peter tonight about going down to Ezekiel's room?" He said, "Peter asked me about it, but I told him no right away". Miss Cathy said, "Did he offer to do anything for you if you let him go to Ezekiel's room?" Mr. Troy nervously said, "No, I just sent him back to bed and told him to go to sleep". Miss Cathy said, "That's not the story I hear from Ezekiel tonight. I hear that Peter performed oral sex on you and then you fell asleep. While you were sleeping, the boys went into Ezekiel's room to have sex. When I got here tonight you were sleeping like you were at home in your bed. Finish your report and go home, you are done for the day. Someone will contact you tomorrow about what's going to happen with this mess"...

Mr. Troy didn't say anything; he just grabbed all this stuff and walked downstairs. After talking to Jonah and the rest of the boys, her mind was made up about what happened on the unit. There was no doubt in her mind that the kids were telling the truth about Mr. Troy...

Mr. Derek asked me, "Did you know about Peter and Ezekiel having a relationship on the unit?" I said that as far as I know, they were just friends. Mr. Derek said, "Okay, I got to see what I can do about this mess" and hung the phone up. I wonder how the company is going to cover this up. A few days later the night staff Mr. Troy was fired for sleeping on the job. There was no mention of the orgy in the Incident Report. It was like it never happened, but it will be in my notes…**"Believe in Change"**

Chapter 18

"House Sitting"

*S*ister Lucy, the "CEO" of the company has been working at God's Love Institute for over 30 years. She has a Doctorate Degree in Theology from a nearby college. She looks very good for her age, which I would guess to be early or mid 50's. She has short black hair, average height and weight. I have only seen her a few times since I have been here and each time she was dressed in a black Nun's outfit. She was the only person on campus who wore one, which made her stand out a lot when she was out of her office. She is the person that everyone in this company answers to and she only answers to God. She wears a Nun's outfit, but from what I understand she is a shrewd business woman...

In my opinion she has forgotten about the welfare of the children and it's all about the money now. This company is making a lot of money, but the kids aren't getting quality work from the staff or management. She has to know this by now, but it seems that her only concern is how much profit did the company make this year. She is the twentieth century version of the Nun, not like the caring and loving ones who started this company over a hundred years ago. The company's mission was all about the welfare of the children, now it's the "all mighty dollar". The Nuns of the past would turn over in their graves if they knew what was going on now. I have heard of prisons being more sensitive to their inmates than this place is to the children...

The only time Sister Lucy leaves her large plush office is when the board members come in town to visit or for a board meeting. She would walk them out to the units and hope she didn't see the kids or the staff acting a fool. She would call ahead to the units to make sure it was okay for her and the board members to be walking on campus. If one of the kids was out of control the staff would let Sister Lucy know and she would quickly postpone the walk until later...

The unit always knew when the Sister and the Board members were coming. She made absolute sure everyone on campus knew of the visit because she didn't want to take any chances of getting embarrassed. On these visits, everything was ironically done by the book. The units were unusually clean, the staff had on clean clothes, kids had on new clothes and all the paperwork was done properly. It was like it should be all the time...

So in reality, this company only has to do their jobs twice a year and still make the same money. The company does their job when someone of importance comes around. Something is terribly wrong with this picture!

Sister Lucy lives on campus in a large four bedroom house that is owned by the company. She has her own personal live-in maid who cleans and walks the Sister's dogs everyday. It doesn't cost the Sister anything to live there, even though she probably gets a salary of 500,000 a year, plus expenses. She lives like a precious queen without a care in the world except for how much more money the company can make....

The maid religiously walks the two dogs every morning around 8:00am on the field where the kids play baseball, football and just run and play. Everyday the kids come back inside the units after playing on the field with dog shit on their shoes. I guess the maid doesn't think the kids are important enough for her to bend down and clean up the dog shit up off the field. The staff has complained about the shit, but no one has done anything yet. It's been a few years since the first complaint; I guess they just aren't going to do anything...

"Children on Layaway, it's all about the Money$$$"

The maid is an old white lady in her 70's or 80's; I'm surprise she can still walk considering her age. She has been working for Sister Lucy for 20 years and has never missed a day of work. That's amazing! Now her age has finally caught up with her and she has become ill. She is in the hospital and some of the staff says that her illness is terminal. Now the Sister has to walk her own dog in the morning, plus feed them. She must find this hard because she has never done this before. After a few days of walking and feeding the dogs, she decided to pay a kid named Timothy to do it for her. He had to go to the house twice a day, 8:00am and 5:00pm to feed and walk the dogs. The dogs are females, black mixed breeds named Elisabeth and Virginia. They weigh about 70 pounds each and friendly with everyone, especially the kids. Actually, I believe the dogs are getting better treatment than the children that live in residential living. What does that say about Sister Lucy and this company?

After Timothy had been working for Sister Lucy a few weeks, she decided to give him a key to the house just in case he had to check on the dogs when she wasn't on campus. She had good reason to trust Timothy; he has a perfect record. He has not gotten in any kind of trouble since he has been on campus; which has been five years. He is a white male, 18 years old and on his way to college when he graduates. He is not on any medications and seems to be on his way to becoming one of the few success stories of this company. Everyone is very proud of him and they should be because it is rare to find a kid like him in residential living. I have only met him a few times, but I was very impressed with how well-adjusted he seemed to be. He is one of the bright spots of my experiences here so far because meeting him gave me hope...

The Sister had an emergency at another facility in another city and had to quickly leave town for the weekend. After careful consideration, she decided to trust Timothy with the welfare of her house and dogs. Timothy's unit is St James, which is conveniently only about 50 feet away from the Sister's house. Timothy could see her house from the front porch of St James. His unit has the best boys on campus there; only the best kids get to live at St. James so you have to have a good record to get there. These kids get to have TV's in their room and stereos. They can stay on the phones as long as they want and they get to stay up later at night. All the boys on campus want to live at St. James...

This is considered a "Step down Unit" on campus and every boy's goal is to get to live there. There are usually no more than five or six boys in the unit at one time. These kids need very little supervision and they have earned that right by doing what they are supposed to do over a period of months. Timothy has been at St. James for almost a year and has a perfect record. He is by far the best kid in the unit right now, maybe on the whole campus...

On Friday at the house, Sister Lucy told Timothy what she expected of him and said that she would be back sometime on Monday. Timothy bravely told her that she could count on him and not to worry about a thing. Timothy took the dogs for a walk and when he came back the Sister had already headed to the airport for her flight...

He was proud of himself, the Sister has never trusted any of the kids to watch her precious dogs and house before. Except for the maid who has been with her for 20 years, the Sister never even considered anyone else to watch over her palace...

All the kids on campus was talking about the honor that was bestowed upon Timothy, even the staff were surprised to hear it. The kids have always been curious about what the inside of the Sister's house looked like and so was the staff. Timothy never got to see more than the kitchen where the dogs are usually waiting for him in the morning. He always wondered what the rest of the house looked like, maybe now he will get his chance. Even though Timothy was tempted to take a tour of the house, he fought the feeling and put the dogs in the kitchen. Timothy knew that if he got caught walking around the house he would not be able to explain that to anyone who might come to the door.

Timothy figured that he had time to take a tour later once he is sure the Sister is really out of town...

That evening at 6:00pm, Timothy finally gave in to his overpowering temptation to take a tour of the Sister's house. The first room he wanted to see was the elusive living room. While walking around the living room he noticed a large bar located in the corner of the large room. The bar is about 15 feet long with seven brown leather bar stools in front. The sides and front of the bar is cover in brown leather and the surface is brown wood. Behind the bar is a large glass cabinet full of assorted liquors and wines. Timothy went behind the bar to get a closer look and also to see if the cabinet was locked. He tried to open the cabinet doors, but they were locked and he would need a key to open them. He was curious to see just how much the Sister really trusted him, which is why he wanted to see if the doors were open...

There must be at least 50 bottles of liquors and wines in the cabinet, if not more. Timothy was wondering why the Sister who is a Nun would have such a large quantity of liquor in her house anyway. Nuns are not supposed to be drinking alcohol, at least that's what he thought. He found all four of the bedroom doors locked also. The door to the basement was also locked and the inside door to the garage. Everything seemed to be locked up tight. This disturbed Timothy a little because he felt like the Sister didn't trust him enough to leave the doors unlocked. The kitchen cabinets and refrigerator were full of goodies, but Timothy knew better than to mess with the Sister's food...

After an hour of roaming around the large house, he decided that he seen enough. He feed and walked the dogs; then he took them back to the house. Both dogs quickly fell asleep on their pillows in the hallway at the bottom of the stairs. They opened their eyes briefly as Timothy cautiously and quietly made his way out the front door. Timothy had been out the unit for two hours, but none of the staff questioned him about it. They knew where he was supposed to be and that all they cared about. Timothy was a little disappointed because everything was locked up and he expected to see more of the house...

It wasn't long before Timothy anxiously told the other kids about all the liquor at the Sister's house. They didn't believe him because they also believe that Nuns don't drink alcohol. He continued to explain what the bar looked like and how many bottles of liquor he saw. They still didn't believe a word he said because they couldn't picture all the liquor in a Nun's house. All the kids left the room except a kid named Mark, who listened intensely to every word that came out of Timothy's mouth. Mark is a six-foot three African American juvenile who comes from the worst part of the town. He has been using drugs and alcohol since the age of ten. He has been in this system off and on for six years. Mark is 16 years old now with a drug addict for a mother and no father in his life. He is trouble just waiting for an opportunity to happen. Mark earned the right to be at St. James because for the last six months surprisingly he has done everything that he was supposed to do. He has only been in this unit for a few weeks now. His room is right next to Timothy's room...

The kids go in and out each other's rooms all the time, even though they are not supposed to. This is just another example of the staff not doing their jobs because even though they live at St. James, these kids need rules and regulations. All kids, no matter where they are living need structure and regulation in their lives. This is a serious mistake that the company and staff seem to make with these children. Children want structure and security in their lives. Their backgrounds have been filled with uncertainty and insecure living styles. They are ready to embrace a secure, loving living environment. This company is failing the kids on their basic needs and wants. Every strong foundation starts with the basics. These children are going to need strong foundations to deal with the realities of life when they turn 18 and leave God's Love Institute...

After the staff fell asleep as usual (1:00am), Mark quietly went into Timothy's room and stole the Sister's house keys. The keys were sitting on Timothy's dresser in plain sight so they were not hard to find. He didn't expect anyone to have the nerve or stupidity to steal the Sister's keys. He always slept like a well-feed baby because he was very comfortable at St. James. A fire alarm would have to go off to wake up Timothy, that's how well he slept...

There was only one staff who worked at night; his name is Mr. Darzel. All the kids know that he sleeps the whole night. It is easy for the kids to know when Mr. Darzel is sleeping because he snores and looks like a large well fed gorilla. If they wanted to sneak out, it would be easy for them because only the smell of fried food would probably wake him up...

Usually the boys would just sneak over to the girl's unit or the girls would sneak over to see them a few nights a week. Sex was not a problem for these kids because staff fortunately slept most of the time. They probably got more sex than the staff and the staff get to go home after work...

Mark noticed that Mr. Darzel's cell phone was sitting in its charger, so he decided to take it with him in case he wanted to make some free unmonitored phone calls. It only took Mark five minutes to get all this done. He had planned for two girls to meet him outside. The girl's staff is also usually sleeping around this time so it won't be a problem for girls to get out of the unit. Their names are Nehemiah and Esther from the unit next to St. James, which is called Sandy Hall...

They had been planning this night every since they heard about the Sister leaving town and giving Timothy the keys to her house. Mark met the girls outside and said with a big smile, "I got the keys, let the fun and games begin". The girls smiled and quietly followed him towards the Sister's house...

"Believe in Change"

Chapter 19

"Party like a Rock Star"

Mark told the girls to wait outside while he got rid of he dogs in the house. He wasn't sure how the girls would act if the dogs came near them and he did not want to take any chances. All the kids on campus knew the dogs and both dogs are very friendly, but he didn't know if the girls liked the dogs. The dogs love to play with the kids, who love to play with the dogs. When Mark got the door open, both dogs were waiting patiently at the door. He gently rubbed each dog on the head and said calmly, "Come on, let's go for a walk". The dogs ran out the door pass the girls and headed towards their favorite spot. They ran towards the field where they love to run and play everyday. Mark followed closely behind the dogs and after a few minutes he left them playing in the field by themselves...

He quickly ran back to where the girls were waiting patiently and said with excitement in his voice, "Let's get this party started". Both of the girls smiled and said, "It's about time". The dogs didn't even notice that Mark left them or didn't seem to care. They were to busy playing and shitting all over the field. He told the girls that the coast was clear as he was looking at his watch to see how much time they had to party. Mark said in a serious voice, "It is 2:00am now, we have to be back at our units before 7:00am before the morning staff comes to work. My cousin Anthony is on his way with some good weed for us to smoke. We are going to have some crazy fun tonight, let's get this party started"...

The lights were already on inside the house so Mark didn't have to worry about seeing inside the house. The downstairs lights were always left on for the dogs to see at night. The Sister doesn't have to pay for electricity so that wasn't any big deal to her to waste the electricity. Mark and the girls went straight to the bar to see if they could get it open. He had wisely brought a screwdriver with him to open the locks to the bar, but he wasn't having any luck...

The reason Mark brought a screwdriver with him is because he remembered that Timothy had said the bar was locked. 15 minutes later and getting pissed off; he kicked the glass out in frustration. The sound of broken glass filled the house as pieces shattered across the floor. This worked so well that he took his shoe off and knocked all the glass out of the bar. Glass was all over the floor, but they didn't care as long as they could get to the liquor that their taste buds had been patiently waiting for all week...

He was like a drug addict trying to get a hit of crack cocaine after being locked up for 90 days. The girls were just watching in amazement as Mark loudly banged all the glass out of the cabinets like there was gold behind the glass. Mark has no reason to worry about the noise because luckily there is no police or security on campus. The staff slept all night so they wouldn't be a threat to the kid's party. They could have a live rock band on the lawn and still get away with their party plans on this unsecured campus ...

God's Love Institute is considered an "Open Campus", sadly meaning that there are no locked gates or security police to stop anyone from leaving or coming on campus. The company uses that as a selling point to encourage families to enroll their children here. The parents are usually very happy to hear that their kids are not going to be locked up by a gate or behind bars. The staff has never been happy about this being an Open Campus because anyone could come on campus and do anything to them or the kids...

Some of these kids are unfortunately in gangs; if a rival gang wanted to do a drive-by shooting on campus there wouldn't be anything to stop them from killing everyone. If a disgruntled parent wanted to harm a staff, all he/she has to do is drive right up to the unit and shoot the whole unit up...

The company has heard about the concerns of the staff, but don't give a damn. Maybe they will start listening to their concerns when someone gets murdered or shot on this campus. The company apparently is not going to spend any additional money to make the staff feel safe. The staff are just not that important to them; it is amazing that the staff put up with this bullshit. I bet this kind of thinking would change if one of the parents or a gang member goes in the main building and starts shooting the place up. I understand that the staff doesn't have a union, but what is wrong with just fighting for what you believe is right. Like they say in the streets, "Man up or shut up" because I am tired and the company is very tired of hearing the staff complain. The fact is this company does not give a shit about you so shut up and fight for what you think is right! It's all about making the money, not whether the staff is working in a safe environment...

After calling his cousin to let him know that everything was in place; Mark and the girls each quickly grabbed a bottle of liquor and sat on the couch to watch one of the music channels on TV. None of them was concerned with what kind of liquor they were getting ready to drink. They just wanted to drink and drink a lot. Mark called his cousin Anthony on the stolen phone that he proudly had in his pocket. He answered the phone and told Mark that he would meet him at the campus entrance in a few minutes. Anthony is 19 years old and has been in and out of trouble since he was 12 years old. He is in a gang (The Bloods) and has been trying to get Mark to join. Anthony has been faithfully in the gang for four years...

Mark met Anthony at the entrance and got into his car to show him where to park it. They parked the car where all the employees park their cars so it wouldn't be too conspicuous.

Anthony smiled and said, "I got the bomb weed, do you got the girls?" Mark said, "The girls are at the house waiting on us and their ready to party and fuck". Mark told Anthony that they have a whole bar full of liquor. We got weed, a bunch of liquor, a big ass crib and plenty of good pussy, let's do this!! Let's party like a Rock Star". When they walked inside the house they were surprised and a little confused at what was going on...

Nehemiah and Esther were naked and on the couch making passionate love together. Mark had heard about the girls making love to each other in the girl's units, but he has never actually seen it before. This behavior is a form of institutionalism that some of the girls go through while in residential living. This doesn't mean that the girls are gay; it is just something that they see other girls doing so they try it. Most of the time when they are released the girls go back to dating boys again...

The liquor bottles that the girls were drinking from were half empty now. They must have been drinking the liquor like it was water after Mark went to get his cousin. He could not have been gone for more than 15 minutes. What a difference a couple more swallows of liquor can make in a person. When Mark left both girls had all their clothes on and were watching music videos on TV. Now 15 minutes later they are making crazy love together...

The girls were so engrossed into what they were doing that they didn't even know anyone was watching them. Mark and Anthony reluctantly sat down at the bar to try to figure out their next move. They started drinking some liquor and smoked some weed while they were thinking and watching the girls. The girls were so passionate about making love that Anthony got excited, but he also was getting a little concerned. He said in a curious voice, "Mark are these bitches gay? Are we going to get some sex tonight or not?" Mark said, "Man don't worry about what these bitches are doing, I have made love to these girls too many times for them not to like boys also". Anthony smiled and

Said, "I want to get some sex while there is still some sex left. The way them girls is licking and sucking on each other they might run out of juices soon". Mark said, "What are we waiting for cousin, let's get to it"...

The girls didn't make any attempt to stop the boys from having sex with them. As a matter of fact, they enjoyed having sex with the boys just as much as they enjoyed having sex with girls. Mark and Anthony took turns making love to each girl without any resistance from them. In between having sex, they were drinking and smoking weed together. After a few hours of heavy drinking and smoking weed, everyone except Anthony passed out in a drunken coma. Anthony was a professional, he drinks and smokes weed everyday; this was nothing new for him because his body is used to this kind of alcohol and drug abuse. He noticed that it was 6:00am and time for him to get the hell off of campus before the sun came up...

He knew that it wouldn't be a good idea to get caught here with two naked minor girls who smell like alcohol and marijuana. Especially since he is on probation right now and he would get sent straight to jail again. He tried to wake Mark and the girls up, but they were too drunk to move...

Anthony was concerned because he didn't want his cousin to get in trouble, but there was nothing else he could do. Time was quickly running out and he had to get away from this situation...

He got his car and backed it up to the house so that he could fill his trunk with the rest of the liquor. He couldn't get all the bottles in there and knew better than to put them in the front seat or rear seat of the car. He was going to take the TV, but it was too big to fit in the car. He saw the Sister's digital camera sitting on the bar and decided to leave some memories on the camera for her...

Anthony pulled Nehemiah over to where Mark was lying and put her mouth on his penis. He rolled Esther in between Nehemiah's legs and pushed her face into her vagina. This picture looked like one big orgy was going on at the Sister's house. He began taking pictures from all kinds of angles like he was a professional photographer. He must have taken about 20 pictures, but he made sure that none of the pictures showed Mark's face. He didn't want to get him into deeper trouble by having his face on this film...

He found a portrait of the Sister and her dogs on the wall and placed it between the two girls. Anthony laughed out loud as he proudly took that last picture. He could only imagine what would go through the Sister's mind when she got this film developed. He put the camera back where he found it and made sure he wiped his finger prints off everything in the house. He calmly shut the door behind him and rushed to his car to make his getaway. While he was driving off campus, the morning staff was driving on campus; late as usual and without a care in the world. He waved good morning to the staff as he sped by without any fear that they might suspect who he was. They probably thought he was one of the night staff leaving...

The daylight staff for St. James arrived at 7:20am. There is two staff who worked daylight on the weekends, Miss Shirley and Mr. Bill. They casually went upstairs together after they greeted each other. Mr. Darzel was asleep as he usually is so that didn't surprise them. Miss Shirley sharply kicks him in his foot and says "Go home sleepy". He wakes up slowly and then starts looking for his cell phone. Miss Shirley meticulously checks all the kid's rooms to make sure everyone is where they are supposed to be. She always checks the rooms when she arrives because she knows that Mr. Darzel sleeps all night. If any of the kids are missing, then that falls on the nightshift. It is their responsibility to figure out where the child is if one is missing. If they can't do that, then they have to notify the authorities of a runaway child. Miss Shirley noticed that Mark's room was empty and asked Mr. Darzel where he was. He said nervously, "He is supposed to be in his room; maybe he's in the bathroom"...

Miss Shirley slowly goes over to the bathroom and hollers loudly for Mark. There is no response to her voice. Mr. Darzel quickly goes in the bathroom and finds no one. He went into every room and anxiously checked underneath all the beds. Mark is nowhere to be found in the whole unit. Miss Shirley said, "When was the last time you checked the rooms last night? Darzel just stood there confused as he scratched his head. He seemed more concerned in finding his precious cell phone...

Miss Shirley angrily said, "You better call the police and start the damn paperwork for a runaway". Mr. Bill calmly said, "Yeah, we need to do something right now. Mark could be in West Virginia by now". The phone suddenly rang and Mr. Bill rushed to answer it trying not to let the person on the other end hear the fear in his voice. It was the staff from Sandy Hall saying that two of their girls were missing...

Miss Shirley said sarcastically, "So we got one kid missing and we don't know how long he has been gone. This is really fucked up"!! Mr. Darzel said, "I think Mark took my fucking cell phone with him because I can't find it anywhere". Miss Shirley said curiously, "Do you at least have your damn wallet and car keys or do we also have to worry about them?" Mr. Darzel said "Yes, what are we going to do about this mess?" Before anyone could answer, Timothy ran out of his room hysterically and said, "Someone took my keys, I looked all over the place". Mr. Bill said to Miss Shirley and Mr. Darzel, "I bet you Mark took the keys. I wonder if he and the girls are at the Sister's house right now". Miss Shirley loudly said to Mr. Darzel, "You lost Mark; you better try to find him before I call the police"...

Mr. Darzel called Sandy Hall and told the night staff Miss Patty that he thinks that he knows where the girls and Mark are hiding at. He told her to meet him in five minutes downstairs so they could walk over to check it out. Miss Shirley said, "Let us know soon because we have to notify the police. You aren't going to get my ass in trouble because you can keep your damn eyes open at night"...

When they got to the Sister's house, they noticed that the door was partially open and they could hear the TV playing loudly. They can smell marijuana seeping out the door. Mr. Darzel walked in first; he was amazed at what he saw laying around the Sister's living room...

Miss Patty, a 25 year old white girl said, "What in the hell is this?" Miss Patty walks over to where the girls are laying and begin firmly shaking them awake. All the kids slowly woke up and slowly put their clothes on. Mr. Darzel found his cell phone lying next to Mark. Mr. Darzel uses his cell phone to call St. James to tell Miss Shirley that he had found the kids. Miss Patty helped get the two girls dressed and took them back to their unit. Mr. Darzel angrily asked Mark, "Where are the Sister's dogs?" Mark said, still half asleep "I don't know, I left them out in the field last night"...

Fed up with the bullshit, Mr. Darzel violently punched Mark in his face as hard as he could. He fell to the floor and cut his hand on some glass. Mr. Darzel viciously kicked him in his side saying, "If you ever fucking take something from me again, I'm going to kill your dumb ass". He kicked him one more time for good measure. Mark didn't even try to fight back; he was still too drunk and probably wasn't feeling any pain yet...

When they got back to the unit, Mr. Darzel explained to Miss Shirley what he found at the Sister's house. After listening intensely to what he said Miss Shirley said, "We better call the Supervisor Miss Ronda so she can make a decision on how to handle this mess. There might be some information that this company may not want everyone to know...

"Believe in Change"

Chapter 20

"The Cover Up"

Mark staggered back to the unit as Mr. Darzel followed closely behind him. He was going through his cell phone as they made their way to the unit. He was trying to see how many calls Mark made and who he called. Mr. Darzel found a lot of phone numbers that he didn't know who they were...

Just as Mark walked upstairs to his room, Timothy quickly came to his door and asked him where his keys were. Mark shouted back angrily, "I don't know what in the hell you are talking about asshole. You better leave me the fuck alone; I am not in the mood for your bullshit". Mr. Darzel calmly told Timothy, "I have the keys; I found them on the floor of the Sister's house". Timothy said in a concerned voice, "I need to go and feed the dogs and take them for a walk". Mr. Darzel said, "Don't worry about that now, the dogs are gone, but hopefully they will come back later". Timothy said hysterically, "Oh my God, I'm going to be in trouble because the dogs are my responsibility". Miss Shirley said, "It's not your fault that Mark stole the keys. The Sister will understand when we explain it to her". Timothy ran to his room crying and saying, "I'll never be trusted again by the Sister or anyone else"...

He was right, trust is something that Timothy had to earn and now he has to earn trust again. That's shameful, but that is how life is to everyone. None of the staff is really worried about Timothy's concerns right now. The biggest worry now is how the Sister is going to react to what happened at her beautiful home...

The Night Coordinator Miss Cathy was off so the supervisor of all the girl's units Miss Ronda was called by Mr. Darzel and he gave her all the slimy details. She was at the unit 30 minutes after the call because that's how upset she was. After getting to the unit and hearing his story again, she told Mr. Darzel that he is suspended until further notice. She told him that they had to figure all this mess out and she would give him a phone call when they do. He didn't even try to defend what happened because he knew that there was no defense for what happened on his shift...

Miss Ronda advised all the staff not to say anything under any circumstances about what happened to anyone else. She didn't even want the other staff on campus to get wind of this incident. News like this spreads like the leaves in the autumn time in Hopesville. This campus can be called "Gossip City"; everyone knows everything about everyone. Here are some examples of gossip that I have heard since I have been here: Mr. Derek has been having a sexual relationship with the Director of Residential Miss Lisa for years. That is probably how he gets away with not doing his job. Both of them have been stealing the company's money for years. Many of the staff is having sex with each other all over campus, usually in the units. Staff has been cheating the company on the time clocks for years, which probably add up to millions of dollars stolen. Racism runs rampant throughout this organization from the top-down, which is why you see very few blacks in positions of power in this organization. That is just a few of rumors that seem to have some truth to them...

Miss Ronda couldn't believe what she read in Mr. Darzel Incident Report. She immediately walked over to the Sister's house to see for herself if it was as bad as he wrote on the report. Miss Ronda was astounded because it was really bad, the bar was destroyed, glass was all over the floor, all the liquor was gone and the dogs were no where to be found...

Ron Howard

The whole house smelled like alcohol and marijuana with a touch of sex to complete the odor. The objects in the house can be fixed or replaced, but her precious dogs cannot. The Sister is going to lose her mind if her dogs are not found before she gets back...

Several Staff members were sent out to search for the dogs. Finally after two hours they found them wandering around in the nearby neighborhood hungry and dirty. The two dogs were happy to see someone that knew who they were. The dogs quickly leaped into the God's Love Institute van without hesitation...

By 12:00pm every Supervisor and Director was on campus having a meeting about the incident. There was fear and tension throughout the meeting that was led by Miss Lisa. The meeting lasted until 3:00pm because there was a lot of blame being thrown around; no one was safe from getting fired. At the meeting they decided to hire a professional cleaning company to clean the Sister's house. They wanted to make sure that it was done correct. They took the house watching job off of Timothy because that was the only way they could be sure the keys would not be stolen again. They had Maintenance come in to repair the Sister's bar and anything else that was broken. Maintenance weren't too happy with coming in because they don't usually work on the weekends...

No one could figure out where the entire stock of the Sister's liquor was at. They didn't believe that the kids could have drunk all the liquor in a few hours. All the units on campus were meticulously checked, but no liquor could be found. This was of great concern to management because they didn't want liquor on campus with the children. A lot of the children on campus have drug and alcohol problems so it would not be good to have bottles of liquor floating around the campus...

Mark and the girls were adamantly saying that there wasn't any liquor at the house, but management knew better than that. They thought about buying some more liquor and wine, but they decided to wait and let the Sister handle that. There wasn't

135

much time to make this right because the Sister will be home Sunday night around 8:00pm...

Miss Lisa, (The Director of Residential Living) decided that they would tell the Sister everything that happened except the part about the kids having sex in her house. They couldn't prove that the kids had sex, but since they were all naked, there was probably a good chance they did...

She told Miss Ronda that Mr. Darzel and Miss Patty needed to be fired immediately. She went on to say that if anyone is caught sleeping from now on; they will be fired on the spot. This kind of stuff would never happen if the Night Coordinator Miss Cathy had been doing her job by making sure the night staff is not sleeping. There should be a Supervisor on night shift, but the company is too cheap to pay for one. It is cheaper to have a (Bucket of Rocks) like Miss Cathy to do the same job for less money. The word on campus is that Miss Cathy only has a G.E.D. Miss Cathy doesn't complain, she is just happy to be a coordinator with her educational background...

Sunday evening (6:00pm), the Sister's house was cleaned up after a lot of arduous work. The only thing that was different is that there wasn't any liquor in the bar. Management was very happy and pleased with the way the Sister's house looked and smelled. No one would be able to tell that a wild orgy with drugs and alcohol happened not too long ago. It is amazing what a little bit of soap and water and some strong chemicals will do to evidence...

The Story about the incident was all over campus two hours after it happened. Probably all over the town thanks to Mark's cousin and his big braggadocio mouth. Miss Ronda picked the Sister up at the airport and drove her to the house. She explained everything to the Sister as they drove. She was pissed about what she heard and told Miss Ronda that she wanted to see all the supervisors tomorrow morning in her office at 9:00am. Before Miss Ronda left that night, the Sister asked her for the extra keys to her house...

I don't think she will seriously trust any more kids with the keys to her house anytime soon. The dogs were very happy to see the Sister after the day they went through eating out of garbage cans in strange neighborhoods. It would be ironic if one or both of the dogs end up pregnant. That would really put the icing on the cake for the Sister...

I personally don't know what the Sister expected when she decided to hire all of these idiots who worked for her. Now I guess it's coming back to haunt her and she deserves every minute of this pain. This is the kind of pain that children have to deal with every day...

The meeting didn't last long that next morning; the Sister was brief and right to the point with what was on her mind. She said, "I want all the paperwork concerning what happened to disappear; I don't want anyone to know about the kids getting drunk off of my liquor. The only things that I want put in the incident report is that the kids ran and was caught hiding in the gym 30 minutes later. This is the story that I want written up and I better not see anything else. Make sure the staff that was responsible for watching these kids never ever comes back on this campus". Everyone knew better than to question the Sister's decision so they hurried out of her office while they still had their jobs...

The Sister knew that if this got out to the families or the public it would be hard to explain. This was a very smart move because it was determined later Monday at 2:00pm that all three of the kids had a mild case of alcohol poisoning. All the kids had to do blood and drug screens when they came back to the units after running. This is standard procedure when a kid runs or goes on a home visit. There was also marijuana found in their systems...

Several months later everything has quieted down and now it's time for the Sister to have the "Annual Company Fundraiser" for the board members and potential donators. This is an opportunity for the company to show and explain all the great things it does for the children with the donated money it receives. Anyone who comes to the fundraiser is expected to donate $300 to enjoy the festivities. This event is very special for the company because it also attracts potential donators to the organization. The company goes all out to impress everyone at these events; money is not an issue for them because they realize that it takes money to make money...

They have the best foods, best entertainment, the best hotels and the biggest halls in Hopesville. This is considered a "Black Tie Event", so everyone is dress to impress. A lot of money is spent, but a lot of money is usually made also. It is not unusual for there to be as many as 400-500 people at the event. The vast majority of the people that come to these events are affluent white professionals with a lot of money. This is just great publicity for the company and the children which generate tons of money...

The owners of some local professional teams come, which include football, baseball and hockey. Some of the athletes show up sometimes, which in turn brings the local news out to take pictures and do interviews. But mostly, it's just the owners of the teams that actually show up...

The Sister knows how important the Fundraiser is and takes it very personal. She is usually involved in every detail of putting the event together. This represents her organization and her honorable and prestigious name. This event is usually held during the summer months when the kids are out of school...

The company proudly puts together slideshows of all the things the kids did during the past year. The showing of the picture slides is always the joyous highlight of the event. People look forward to seeing the happy smiling faces on all the children. This is the reward that they are looking forward to seeing after making their generous donations every year. Especially the Sister and the Board Members of God's Love Institute, this is what needs to be seen to continue to make more money for the company...

Every year there is always someone to take pictures at every event the children go to. This year the Sister proudly took the Christmas party pictures on her trusted digital camera. All the pictures are supposed to be edited before they are added to the slideshow. However this year all the pictures were edited except the Sister's pictures...

The Human Development Department is in charge of editing the pictures, but they didn't think they had to worry about the Sister's pictures. The Sister is known for taking great pictures. Everyone knows that she takes a lot of pride in her contribution to the slideshow...

Human Development is in charge of putting all the events together for the children such as picnics, amusement parks and many more activities throughout the year. Human Development receives an assortment of donations from the public. Some examples are: Free golfing outings, free massages, free hotel rooms and a lot of money. Most of the donations can't even be used by the children, but the company accepts them anyway. They don't offer any of the donations that the children can't use to the staff so I wonder where they go...

I guess the company would have to give a damn about the morale of the staff on campus to give away some of their precious donations to the people who actually do the work. I believe that the company should offer some of the donations to the staff to help raise the moral on campus. I have not met any staff on campus who thinks that this company gives a damn how they feel yet...

The night of the event always starts with a prayer and then the Sister thanking everyone for coming. After 30 minutes of her talking, she starts the slideshow of all the things the kids did with all the generous donations. The show starts with showing the kids at the local amusement park. There are plenty of smiles throughout the audience and some laughter as they watch the kids enjoy themselves. Next the kids are shown at the annual summer cookout eating a lot of great barbeque and playing a variety of games. Finally it's time for the slideshow of the Sister's pictures that she so proudly took at the Christmas party. The audience started watching the pictures slowly change from one happy kid to another...

The children were joyously opening up gifts and eating food. There is happiness permeating throughout the room now. Everything is going great, what could possibly go wrong? The crowd was applauding loudly at almost all of the pictures now. There was happiness and joy throughout the whole building. From out of nowhere silence abruptly entered the room followed by shock and disgust on the faces of the audience. All eyes in the room were locked in disbelief to the slideshow. The crowd was frozen; they looked like statues frozen in time. What once was earlier a joyous occasion had now turned into a disaster of an incredible magnitude...

On the 15 foot screen is pictures of naked teenage kids in various sexual positions. The pictures were from the party that Mark and the girls had a few months ago at the Sister's house. The pictures continued to change as the Sister rushed over to pull the plug out of the wall to put a stop to this mental torture. She awkwardly tripped and fell several times trying to get to the plug. She looked like a football player trying to get through the line of scrimmage...

Shouts were coming from the audience, "Turn that filth off". It only took 45 seconds to get it off, but it seemed like an eternity for the Sister. People had already begun to leave the room, they were outraged and disgusted. The others were sitting there with their heads down in shame wondering how in the hell could something like this happen. The Sister announced to the crowd that there is some difficulty with the slideshow and some great food will be served shortly...

In spite of what happened, the party still went on. I guess everyone wanted to get their $300 worth of entertainment and the sex scenes were just a bonus. There were whispers in every corner of the party about what was seen on the slideshow...

140

That following week the company sent out heartfelt apologizes to everyone who was at the party. They blamed everything on an outside company that they supposedly contracted to put the slideshow together. They said that there would be lawsuits pending once their lawyers figure out what terribly went wrong. Since God's Love Institute has been in this business for over 100 years, they eventually were forgiven by everyone. It certainly helps when the name of your company is called God's Love Institute… **<u>"Believe in Change"</u>**

Chapter 21

"The Hostile Environment"

I recall when Mr. Douglas had to work a week as the "On-call supervisor". Anybody who works for management has to work at least one week of on-call duties every two or three months. This is something that you have to do in conjunction with your regular duties on campus. When you're the On-call, you are unfortunately on duty 24 hours a day and you can get a phone call at any time during that day. This can be a very frustrating job and by the end of the week the unlucky staff is more than ready to turn the On-call job over to the next person...

I remember on a Saturday evening walking around on campus taking a break; I heard a small child crying loudly and it was coming from one of the girl's units. So out of curiosity I walked into the unit to see what was going on and to my surprise I actually saw a two year old African-American girl being carried around by one of the children in the unit. I asked a 13-year-old girl whose baby she was carrying around and her response was "It's my baby mister". I asked the other girls that were downstairs where their staff was and they said that the staff was upstairs supervising the other girls while they take showers. I went to the bottom of the stairs and shouted up and a new staff named Miss Daisy came to the top of the stairs. I asked her if that was her baby and she said yes. I told her that her baby was crying and that she might want to consider coming downstairs to see what's wrong with her. She nonchalantly said, "Oh she's okay, she's just a little hungry right now; the girls are going to feed her something in a few minutes". Needless to say, I was shocked and appalled by the attitude and carelessness of this staff having her two year old child in the unit with troubled youth. I had a serious concern for the child so I decided to call the On-call supervisor who happened to be Mr. Douglas, the Spiritual Director on campus...

At first he thought I was joking and then he became very quiet as if he was trying to regain his composure. He was so upset that he became to curse over the phone. He angrily said, "What in the hell do you mean there is a two-year-old child at the girl's unit? You have got to be shitting me; who in the hell would authorize something like that? Let me call the unit and find out what in the hell is going on; I'll give you a call back". I was a little shock to hear those words coming out of his mouth so easily considering that he is a Spiritual Director and preaches the word of God every Sunday on campus...

He called me back and told me that the staff's supervisor authorized her to work with her child on the unit because they didn't have anyone else to work that shift. The staff told the supervisor that she couldn't come in to work unless she brought her child with her because she didn't have any babysitter and the supervisor agreed to it. This is how desperate the company is to fill shifts...

No matter how desperate the company is; the staff who thought that it was a good idea to bring their two-year-old child to work has to be one of the dumbest and most selfish parents that I have ever met. I doubt if the company knew anything about this agreement between the supervisor and the staff. If something was to happen to that child while on the unit, I could only imagine what would happen to their insurance rates...

Mr. Douglas and myself were mentally traumatized just knowing that there was a two-year-old innocent child on a unit in residential living for troubled youth. It is going to take me some time to get over this, but I know that with the help of God I also will get through this...

In spite of me stepping down from the position of supervisor, the staff is still treating me like I still work for management. In some ways this is good because the staff don't abuse the kids when I'm working, at least not in my presence. I don't get any support or help from the staff if any of the kids are acting-out. This makes working at St. Pauls an unsafe environment for me. We all need to work together as a team to be effective in working with these children. The only team in St. Pauls is the Three Stooges (Curly, Larry, and Moe), that would be alright if this was television. This is real-life and someone could get hurt if we don't watch each other's back. I just have to watch my own back until I get away from this unprofessional unit...

One Sunday morning at 10:00am, I escorted a new kid named Luke downstairs to hopefully relieve some tension between him and his roommate Mathew. Luke has been verbally agitating Mathew constantly all morning. He has been calling him a dick sucker, a faggot and I could tell that Mathew is just about fed up. He is ready to explode and that is what I wanted to avoid. Luke has only been at God's Love Institute for a few days and he has not quite adjusted to how things are done yet. This usually takes about two weeks to assimilate a kid into the program at St. Pauls. These first few weeks takes patience from all the staff. The new kid needs all the help he can get in order to make a smooth transition into this residential living. That is not usually the case; most of the staff on the first day, try to beat the new kid down mentally and physically...

While I had Luke downstairs, two of the Three Stooges (Moe and Larry) decided to take all but three of the kids to the Y.M.C.A off-campus. Mr. Moe and Mr. Larry didn't want to go to the campus church because they thought it was boring for them. I believe the real truth is that they are really Demons and church makes them uncomfortable. They are always looking for any excuse to stay away from the church. If Mr. Douglas questions the staff about not coming to church, they will lie and tell him that they went to a church off campus. If the kids are questioned, they tell the same story because they don't want to get in trouble with the staff. The staff has been known to retaliate

144

against a kid that has snitched on them. This is very frustrating for Mr. Douglas because he gets no support from Management to help resolve this problem...

After 30 minutes downstairs diligently counseling Luke on what I needed him to do, I escorted him back upstairs. When I got upstairs all but three of the kids were lined up in the hallway to go to the Y.M.C.A. Moe had also talked Mr. Stan into going with them, which wasn't anything new because Mr. Stan does everything Mr. Moe tells him. He is a follower and he could be a good leader in my opinion if he applied himself. I'm going to be stuck with Mathew, Luke and Jonah who are probably the worst kids on a unit...

The staff knows the trouble that I'm having with Luke and Mathew, but they don't give a damn. Hopefully I won't have any additional problems and the rest of the morning will be quiet...

As soon as Luke was sure that the other staff had left the building he started talking shit to Mathew again. It is hard to do a restraint properly if there is only one staff so I'm not sure what I want to do about the possibility of these two boys fighting. I'm just going to do whatever I have to do to stop these two kids from killing each other...

I could understand the Staff leaving if everything is quiet; at least that is the way it should be. This makes me think that they are trying to set me up to get hurt. Hopefully I can keep everything under control for a few more hours and get out of this awkward situation...

I cautiously took my three kids down to the kitchen to eat some breakfast; maybe a full stomach will calm them down. Luke is still running his mouth while eating; he is constantly saying negative things about Mathew. My redirections are falling on his deaf ears and I'm getting frustrated with him. I'm tired of waiting on him to shut the fuck up and I know Mathew is ready to jump on him. He is bout 40 pounds heavier than Luke and a little taller. I know Mathew could smash him, but he is trying not to get in trouble because he knows that will affect what level he is on. In this unit the kids are automatically put on level one for a week if they get into a fight...

I'm not sure what the real problem is between them. It might be a racial issue or Luke is just testing Mathew. It is possible that Luke thinks he is White because of his skin color. He looks White, but he is African American. His father is Black and Mathew's mother is White. No one would know his race by simply looking at his skin or the way he talks...

What I feel like doing is letting Mathew beat Luke's ass one good time. I believe that would shut Luke up, but that wouldn't be professionally right. I want to do the right thing for these children no matter how I feel sometimes...

After being in the kitchen for 30 minutes, which seemed like 30 hours to me; I walked all the kids back upstairs to finish cleaning their rooms. I told them that once they get their rooms clean, I will take them to church. Most of the kids are not crazy about going to church, but they'll do almost anything to get out of this building. Even if it is just going to church, the children are generally happy to get out. Lord knows that I need some prayer right now!! The kids definitely need some, besides it always makes Mr. Douglas very happy to see some of St. Paul's kids. I sat down in the hallway as the kids went into their rooms to clean them. Five minutes later to my despair, all hell broke loose in Mathew and Luke's room...

I heard Mathew screaming loudly, "He hit me, don't hit me". I heard heavy objects being thrown and pushed around the room. In a matter of seconds, I sprung to my feet like a cat and ran to their room. Mathew had Luke in a choke hold and both of them had fallen onto Luke's little bed. Mathew was still screaming as he choked Luke's neck tighter, "He hit me Mr. Renaldo; he started it". Luke wasn't saying anything because he was to busy struggling for air as Mathew tried to squeeze the life out of him. He hasn't been this quiet all the morning and now he can hardly breathe. How ironic is that? This amusing thought brought a smile to my face as I went over to the bed to attempt to break the fight up...

Luke is courageously struggling, but he is no match for Mathew's size and strength. I thought about letting them fight a little longer, but I didn't think Luke could last very much longer without air in his lungs...

I got down on the bed and started desperately pulling on Mathew's arms to relieve some pressure on Luke's skinny neck. The harder I pulled, the tighter Mathew squeezed his neck. As I was pulling on Mathew's arms, all I could see was rage and hate in his eyes. I could sense that he really wanted to kill Luke if I let him. I was finally able to break Mathew's grip after five minutes of pulling and pleading with him. He was looking and acting like a madman when he had his arms around Luke's neck. We were all sweating now and tired...

I saw fear and desperation in the eyes of Luke as he swallowed his first complete breath of fresh air since Mathew started choking him. All that cockiness seemed to be a thing of the past after looking at the defeated look on Luke's face. It's amazing what the lack of air will do to a person's attitude and demeanor...

I noticed that Luke had numerous bruises on his neck as I escorted him out to the hallway. I told him to sit on the floor and relax and don't move. I went back in the room and told Mathew to sit on his bed and calm down. He got up slowly and walked to his bed mumbling, "He hit me first Mister". I told Mathew, "I know he started the fight, but right now I just want you to take deep breathes and calm down". He began taking the deep breathes and I walked from the room to check on Luke again. I asked him, "Are you okay, do you need anything?" He said in a scratchy dry voice, "I'm fine, I don't know why you broke the fight up". This comment really pissed me off. I said angrily, "Because Mathew was about to break your fucking neck". After all this bullshit, this little asshole was still talking shit and I couldn't believe it. I walked away from him while I still had some reasonable control over my urges to let Mathew beat on his ass some more...

I checked on Jonah to see how he was doing because I know he heard everything that was going on. He was just lying on his bed calmly reading a magazine as if nothing was happening. I guess he used to hearing this kind of commotion in residential living. He looked up at me and said, "I hope Mathew beat that boy's ass because if he didn't than I will". I guess he was also tired of hearing his mouth all morning. I said with a smile on my face, "When you see Luke's neck, you'll know who won the fight"...

I slowly walked back down the hall and sat down to regain my composure again. I told Luke, "Don't say a damn word to me because I'm not in the mood". He looked at me with a stupid grin on his face and started to say something, but decided that he better not push me any further. He knew by my actions and words that it was finally time to be quiet. I could see that Mathew was already lying across his bed, he was almost sleeping. I guess he was mentally and physically tired from dealing with Luke all morning...

While I was sitting in the chair, I noticed sharp pains in my lower back and my right knee. I must have twisted both of them badly when I was breaking up the fight. I figured that the pain would go away in a few days if I take it easy...

Anytime there is an incident like a fight or restraint, the nurse has to be called shortly after it's over to see if anyone is hurt. The nurse also checks the staff to see if he/she has any injuries. Most of the time the other staff never report this type of incident because they don't want to do the paperwork...

While I was doing the Incident Report, I called the nurse Miss Susan and told her what happened. Miss Susan said that she would be at the unit in about an hour. Unfortunately she had to come all the way from home. She is never happy when she has to drop whatever she is doing and come to campus and deal with these kids. I looked at both boys and the only one that had a mark on them is Luke. He has bruises on his neck and some scratches on his face. I think I got the only real injuries and I wasn't the one who was fighting. How ironic is that!! Where's the justice in that? My lower back and knee is hurting more as time goes on. Something about these injuries doesn't feel right to me. They don't feel like the normal sprains and strains that a staff might get from breaking up a fight...

Everytime that I think about the Stooges leaving me here with these angry kids, I got upset. If there was another staff here when the fight broke out, I probably would not have these injuries; hopefully nothing serious is wrong...

The nurse arrived and checked the boys out first. She found nothing wrong with them other than a few bruises and scratches. She asked me, "How do you feel, are you alright? Where was the other staff when this happened?" I told her, "They left me here to deal with Mathew and Luke by myself. I have some pain in my lower back and right knee". Miss Susan said, "I will write that in my report so expect the company to send you to see the company doctor". She asked me if I thought that I could make it through the rest of the shift. I told her that I would do my best. She walked out the door with a smile on her face and said "Be careful mister". I guess she was happy to be going back home and away from these kids...

Luke was very quiet now which made everyone happy. I guess Mathew had got his attention when he choked the shit out of him. I was happy because I needed some peace and quiet for the rest of the day...

Both my back and knee had swollen up and became very stiff. I could hardly move around without agonizing pain in both areas. If I had to do a restraint now, the kids would be out of luck because I couldn't help them if I tried. I probably should have gone home when the nurse asked could I make it through the rest of the shift. Hopefully the other Staff will be back soon and I can take it easy for the rest of the day...

At 1:00pm, the other staff finally came back to the unit. My three kids were in the TV room sitting and quietly watching one of there favorite programs (Wrestling). I was sitting in the office finishing up on some paperwork on the incident today. Mr. Stan came in the office and asked me how things went between Mathew and Luke after they left. I told him that they got into a fight shortly after you left the unit. He said in a concerned voice, "Did anyone get hurt?" I told him no, I didn't want to give him or the two Stooges the pleasure of knowing that I got hurt...

I sensed the Mr. Stan was sincere about whether anyone got hurt, but I wasn't sure. He wasn't like Mr. Moe and Mr. Larry who I consider devoted and established Child Abusers. I actually believe he has a good heart and he is just badly influenced by that dumb ass Mr. Moe...

Mr. Larry and Mr. Moe didn't say anything to me when they came in the unit; they didn't even look in my direction. They just took their kids upstairs and begin sending them down to Mr. Stan, three at a time to feed them lunch...

I believe that the two Stooges planned on leaving me here alone with the hope that I get hurt dealing with Mathew and Luke; well there plan worked this time. That should make them feel good when they find out about my injuries...

For the rest of the shift I stayed in the office because I didn't want anyone to see me limping around. The Stooges would enjoy seeing me in pain for the rest of my life. God tells me to forgive my enemies and that is what I intend to do. This is a hostile environment for me and I need to be careful. When I get home tonight, I will ask for guidance from God. I will get my answer from my prayers... "**<u>Believe in change</u>**"

Ron Howard

Chapter 22

"The Wounded Soldier"

A few days after my job related injuries, I was sent by the Director of Human Resources to see the company doctor to be examined. The doctor sent me the next day to get x-rays on my lower back and my right knee. The results of the x-rays didn't show anything, so the doctor determined that I had strains and sprains. The company doctor assigned me to light duty from 7 a.m. to 3 p.m. and I had to go to therapy a few days a week...

However I was off from work for 30 days before Miss Kate the "Human Resource Director" called me in for light duty. I don't know why it took her so long to find light duty work for me. I really didn't care; just as long as I get paid...

Psychologically, 30 days off was a blessing because I wasn't ready to deal with this company yet. I have been under a lot of stress trying to deal with the staff at St. Pauls...

The meeting with Miss Kate went well; she seemed sincere in expressing her concern about me getting better. She has been working in the main building for the God's Love Institute for 20 years. As far as I know Miss Kate has never been over to residential living on campus. She is a middle aged white lady with an office in the main building...

She told me that I would be working for her from Monday's through Friday 7 a.m. to 3 p.m. This company didn't really have light duty, but because of their agreement with the insurance carrier they had to offer me light duty or their premiums would go up...

Miss Kate explained what was expected of me as a light-duty employee. She said in a sympathetic voice, "We don't want

151

you working with the kids because the company doesn't want you to get in to another restraint. We don't want you to re-injure your back or knee so we need you to be very careful". I wasn't very happy about not being allowed to work with the kids anymore, but I understood why they didn't want me to participate in any restraints...

For the next two weeks all I did was shred paper and put stamps on envelopes; something that a trained monkey could do. Work was boring, but I dealt with it anyway because I needed to take it easy mentally and physically...

I have been seeing the company doctor once a week since the injury and each time I told him that my back or knee wasn't getting any better. Finally he reluctantly agreed to let me take a MRI on both injuries to get a better view of the injured areas. A week later it was determined that I needed surgery on my knee and I had three herniated disc in my lower back. I wasn't surprised because I knew something was seriously wrong with the knee because it was getting worse. The therapy was more painful each time I went and it was constantly hurting me to walk short distances. I used to dread going to therapy because of the pain that I would have when they were done pulling and pushing on my knee and my back...

The company sent me to see a knee surgeon named Dr. Klein. He wanted to do the surgery in the next two weeks, but I asked him to delay it until after I went to my graduation from the University of Hopesville. After all the sacrifices I made to get my degree in child psychology, there was nothing going to stop me from putting my cap and gown on and making the ceremonial walk to get my degree...

I will graduate in 30 days, so I scheduled the surgery for a week after my graduation. Miss Kate seemed surprised when I told her that I needed surgery on my knee. I guess she didn't think my injuries were that serious or she was hoping that they weren't that serious...

I have been hurt for two months and not one person from residential living checked to see how I was doing. Not even my supervisor Mr. Derek had the decency to give me a call. I remember the last conversation I had with Mr. Derek. He said quietly as we walked down the sidewalk, "No matter what the doctor says, you tell him that you feel fine and you have no limitations because we need you at work". What a selfish and insensitive asshole he is for asking me to disregard my injuries so he wouldn't be short-staffed on the unit...

My graduation was great, Janet and the kids were very proud of me. Everyone was surprised when I first told them I was going back to college. All my friends and family thought I was just joking around. Now I have two degrees, "Child and family Studies" and "Applied Developmental Psychology". No one in my past could have ever imagined me having a college education. My education is extremely important, but it doesn't mean nothing if idiots are the vast majority that work for this company. I'm the first one in my family to ever graduate from college. Hopefully I will be breaking the cycle and it will carry on through my children...

I wanted to have my degree because I believe it will be easier to encourage higher education to the young people that I counsel. I have also written a book documenting my past discrepancies as a kid. This book will be released soon; hopefully the book will encourage and inspire these children to believe in the possibilities of change. I don't know how this company is going to react when they find out about the book. I'm sure they won't be happy when they read about the things that I had to do to get where I'm at right now. I will worry about that later; right now I need to focus on getting better. Right now it's time to deal with the knee surgery...

I had my knee surgery at 7:00am and was at home at 4:00pm the same day. Janet had to help me get around for a few days until I was able to get on my crutches. To my surprise, the company sent me a fruit basket and a card that read, "We wish you a speedy recovery, Sister Lucy". Janet and I were speechless and we didn't know what to say, neither one of us simply just didn't expect anything from this company. One thing that I have learned about this company is to expect the unexpected. Maybe someone in the management really does give a damn about their employees...

10 days after my surgery I went see the surgeon again for a follow-up. He told me that my leg was looking fine and he wanted me to start therapy for a few weeks. He said, "After that we would see about getting you back to full duty"...

Four weeks of therapy and my knee still isn't feeling any better and I don't know why. I told the doctor, but he still sends me back to work full duty. Before I left his office I gave him a piece of my mind. I said, "What kind of doctor are you? You can see that my knee isn't 100%, but you're still signing a paper reading that I can go back to full duty. How much money is workers compensation paying you to do this you fucking asshole?"

I was pissed off and felt like punching him in his face. In my opinion a doctor is someone that you are supposed to be able to count on. If I tell my doctor that I am still not feeling well, then my doctor is supposed to support how I feel and back me up and writing. I painfully limped out of his office and down the hall cursing every step of the way...

God's Love Institute and Workers Compensation have already got my Primary Care doctor to release me to full duty for my back. Workers compensation were constantly calling his office and threatening to take him to court if he didn't release me to full duty for my back injury. This is in spite of the fact that I have three herniated in my lower back. They harassed my doctor to the point that he gave in and said that I could work full duty. He couldn't stand the pressure...

My doctor said that Workers Compensation was threatening him by saying he wasn't a "Back Specialist". This was all done while I was trying to recover from my knee injury. Once workers compensation found out that I needed surgery, they stopped paying for therapy on my back even though it hadn't got any better. Apparently this company would do anything to get me back to full duty. This company doesn't care if I am 100% or not, they just want another body back on the units...

Their insurance rates go higher the longer that I'm on light duty or on workers compensation. I understand why they are pressuring me and my doctors, but they need to consider the employee's point of view. It's all about the money; it has never been about the children or the staff...

The company wanted me to work full duty and start working two 16 hour shifts at St. Pauls on the weekends again. When I heard this from Miss Kate I quickly called Mr. Derek and asked him could I just work two eight hour shifts. I told him that I didn't feel like I could do two 16 hour shifts right now. He said, "If your doctor says that you can work full duty then you have to go back to working your normal 16 hour shifts". I told him okay and as soon as I got off the phone I called my doctor to see if I could get him to help me out. I asked my doctor could he at least change my work status to only working eight hours a day until I'm feeling better. After 10 minutes of persuasion from me he reluctantly agreed and I went to pick up the paperwork...

Janet took it over to Miss Kate at Human Resources and I called Mr. Derek and explained my new status to him. He was pissed just like Miss Kate, but there was nothing they could do about it. Mr. Derek told me that I would be working at St. James on Saturday and Sunday from 3 to 11 this weekend. I was happy that I didn't have to go to St. Pauls again; I simply was not ready to deal with the Three Stooges and all their bullshit...

The kids at St. James are easier to work with and need less supervision. Hopefully I'll have a nice quiet weekend without any restraints. I haven't worked with kids in a residential in five months; I might be a little rusty. I knew my body was not at 100%, but I'll be alright for now if I don't have to do a restraint. I was blessed; I had a nice quiet weekend, I really enjoyed myself at St. James...

I received a phone call at home on Friday from Miss Kate. She said, "We want you to work the night shift, so give Miss Cathy, the "Night Coordinator" a call to see when you can start". I called Miss Cathy 15 minutes later and she said that I couldn't start until Wednesday next week. She said her shift was full and she didn't have a spot for me yet. I knew that grumpy old bitch was lying because Janet told me the night shift is always short...

Most of the time, the kids are sleeping all night so it would be rare to have to do a restraint. The good news is that I wouldn't be working for Mr. Derek or dealing with the Three Stooges anymore. I am sure that the Three Stooges are happy that I'm no longer working at St. Pauls; I might be happier than them. Now they can go back to abusing the kids and stealing money from the company without worrying about me snitching on them...

This should also make Mr. Derek happy because I won't be around to ask him where the unit money is anymore. He can steal the money freely again and he can start buying his fancy suits again. He can also take his girlfriend Miss Lisa to fancy expensive dinners and romantic getaways. The money should be flowing again for Mr. Derek since I'm out of the way. As always, the children in residential living are in my prayers...

"Believe in Change"

Chapter 23

"Curly Strikes Again"

$\mathcal{J}$ scheduled an appointment to see a new Primary Care doctor who hopefully will be a little more considerate to how I say I'm feeling. I worked two night shifts and than saw the new doctor on Friday at 1 p.m. This doctor is a white female named Dr. Tooly; she thoroughly looked at my records and immediately put me back on light duty because of the herniated disc. Dr. Tooly was bewildered by my last doctor's decision to send me back to full duty in spite of my obvious physical condition. She questioned me about why the doctor decided to put me on full duty, but I really didn't have any answers for her. The only thing I could think of was that Workers Compensation must have paid my last doctor off. Dr. Tooley smiled and said, "I am going to get you better and until then you need to be working light duty"...

Those are the words that I long awaited to hear from a doctor. Now I've felt like I had a professional in my corner that really cared about me. My knee was still hurting, but I didn't even have to say anything about it. I immediately informed Miss Kate at Human Resources and she told me to come to work on Monday with my doctor's excuse at 8:00am to 4:00pm. She wanted to meet me at her office so she could tell me where and what I would be doing on light duty...

At the meeting she told me that I would be doing the same things as before (When I was on light duty) except sometimes I would be doing some data entry. I was very pleased that I found a doctor who was willing to back the patient up against these big corporations like Workers Compensation and

God's Love Institute. I guess there are some doctors who can't be pressured or paid off to get the employee back to full duty work when the staff is still injured...

Most of the gossip on campus is shared at the smoking areas. Some staff that doesn't even smoke cigarettes will go there just to hear about what's going on. I could write a book with the stories that are told there. The main smoking area on campus is outside the main building. This is the only legal smoking area, but the staff smoke almost anywhere they want. It's not like the supervisors is really enforcing the smoking policy. Actually, nothing is really enforced on campus...

While at the smoking area, I overheard a story about one of the Three Stooges (Mr. Curly). Here is how the story went: One staff said, "Did you hear that Mr. Curly was child-lined again for choking the shit out of a kid named Jonah. He viciously choked him from the ball field all the way up to St. Paul's front porch. Once Mr. Curly got him on the porch, he put both hands firmly around Jonah's neck to choke him even harder. He lifted him 3 feet in the air as Jonah struggled wildly to get loose. The whole thing started after Curly lost his temper when Jonah threw an empty milk crate towards him while he was playing cards with the other staff"...

The only reason that Mr. Curly got Child-lined was because he was seen by kids and staff choking Jonah. Mr. Derek had to child-line him to cover his back, he had no other choice. There were too many people that were a witness to this crime to even consider covering it up...

After the Child-line paperwork was initiated, Mr. Derek put Mr. Curly in another unit (St. Johns) while the investigation was being conducted. I think that's bullshit because a staff shouldn't be working with any kids until the child abuse case is resolved. God's Love Institute is a cheap ass company and just don't give a damn! The company's biggest concern is that they have a body on the units. There really shouldn't be any investigation because the facts and witnesses are there...

Mr. Curly should have been fired that same day as the incident. Especially with his past history of abusing children that spans over 10 years...

There is talk from Mr. Derek and the company that he will get fired this time; I'll believe that when I see it. Nothing this company does anymore is a surprise to me, but that will be...

After few days into the investigation Mr. Curly heard from other staff on campus that he might get fired. He decided to fake like he was hurt from when Jonah threw to milk crate at him. He told the company doctor that his side was hurting because the crate hit him there so the doctor put him on light duty with me. Now I have to work with this fool again. My back hurts, my knee hurts and now I have to deal with this child abuser. I get sick to my stomach just thinking about how many poor kids he has hurt. I tried to avoid him, but most of the time we have to work together on light duty...

Mr. Curly is very good at pretending that he likes me. He always has of fake ass smile on his face to mask his true feelings. He certainly had me fooled at first because I thought he was a God-fearing man and a deacon at his church. I'm sure Mr. Curly has a lot of people fooled, but he can't fool God. There is no rational excuse for what he did to that poor kid. He choked him hard enough to leave finger marks on his neck and he still gets to work here...

Jonah is not complaining to anyone so that's a good thing for Mr. Curly. Mr. Derek still has to do something because so many people know about it and they expect something to happen. Mr. Curly knows that the company will not fire him while he is he has a suspected job-related injury. I am sure that's his strategy to get the heat off for what he did to Jonah. I believe he will work this light duty job until the outcome of the Childline is determined...

A few days later another staff named Mr. Edwin joined me and Mr. Curly on light-duty at the main building. He broke his hand in a restraint a few days ago and the company rushed him back to work light duty. He has been working for God's Love Institute for about 10 years. He is a 32-year-old African-American male who is very familiar with how Mr. Curly works and the reputation he has on campus. I have only worked with Mr. Edwin a few times when he was working overtime at St. Pauls on the weekends. I never had any problems with him and he seemed like a nice person; at least to me he was. I have never seen him mistreat the children and that is very important to me...

He told me a funny story about the time Mr. Curly stole his lunch from the refrigerator at St. Pauls. Mr. Curly is notorious on campus for stealing the children's and other staff's food. The story went like this: On this particular day, Mr. Edwin brought some of his wife's fried chicken to work. He loves his wife's chicken very much and speaks very highly of it to everyone. He said, "That day I have been thinking about that chicken all morning. Lunch time just couldn't come fast enough for me; I was looking at my watch every 15 minutes. I was so hungry that the hands on my watch was starting to look like chicken wings to me. At around 11:00a.m., Mr. Curly came upstairs with a plate full of fried chicken and sat down next to me. His chicken was looking and smelling good, but I was going to wait until 12:00 p.m. to eat my own delicious home fried chicken. Mr. Curly didn't even offer me a piece of his chicken, but that's alright because I have my own downstairs in the refrigerator. I am really hungry now after smelling and looking at Mr. Curly's chicken. 30 minutes later as Mr. Curly was gobbling down his last bite of chicken he looked at me and said with chicken grease still dripping down his lips, "Boy your wife sure can fry some good chicken". Curiously I asked him, "How do you know about my wife's chicken?" He smiled and said, "Because I just ate some that I found in the refrigerator downstairs". I couldn't believe what this fucking old man just told me. I thought he was playing with me so I asked him again. I said in a loud voice, "Are you telling me that you just ate my chicken that I had in my lunch bag downstairs?" I expected him to say no, I'm just messing with you. He smiled at me again and said, "I thought you brought that chicken to share with all the staff because we share over here. Everyone else that brings food over here shares it with everyone else. I'll bring you some chicken the next time my wife cooks some and will be even". I didn't say anything to him; I quickly went downstairs to see if he really ate my chicken. I looked in my bag and to my chagrin all four pieces of my precious chicken was gone. I was furious, I couldn't believe that this motherfucker had the nerve to steal my food and eat it in front of me. I didn't know whether he was trying to play with my manhood or if he just was that damn ignorant. I was going to find out even if that meant that we was going to roll across the floor fighting. I was on my way back up stairs because I was ready to fight him if he still had the same attitude. I was ready to beat the shit out of him or get my ass beat. My wife's chicken is worth fighting over!! On my way up the stairs I ran into Mr. Stan and luckily he was able to calm me down. I don't know what would have happen that day and Mr. Stan didn't help me calm down. Every since then, I hide my food from this thieving crook who calls himself a Deacon". The way he told the story to me made it sound funny, but there's really nothing funny about stealing another man's food. Especially his wife's good old fried chicken...

Three weeks after Mr. Curly abused Jonah, there was a hearing and to my surprise he was exonerated of any wrong-doing. I just knew for sure that Mr. Curly was going to get fired this time. He wasn't allowed to work at St. Pauls anymore because of all the negativity he has created with the children. That is the good news; however the bad news is that he is still going to be able to work with children. Mr. Derek curiously made Mr. Curly work at St. Johns from 7 a.m. to 3 p.m. Monday through Friday. I don't know what genius came up with this strategy. I guess the company didn't want Mr. Curly working around Jonah anymore. The ages of kids at St. Johns range from 6 - 12. When Mr. Derek put Mr. Curly there, it was like putting a wolf in with some kittens. Those kids aren't going to have a chance with a 225 pound predator like Mr. Curly...

After Mr. Curly got the good news about the Child-line, he miraculously got better. The milk crate injury that he said he had suddenly and coincidentally disappeared from his body. It was like a miracle!! So instead of him getting fired or punished for choking Jonah, he was rewarded with a daylight job with smaller kids to prey on. This company still continues to amaze me with their support of a known child abusers. What does this man have on this company that stops them from firing him? If I did decide to write a book about this company, who will believe even half of the stories about this place. What I'm seeing here is even hard for me to fathom and I'm seeing it with my own eyes...

Janet told me about this elderly African-American female staff named Miss Maria who got beat up by one of the girls at St. Micah. Miss Maria is at least 65 years old and works to supplement her income like a lot of senior citizens today. She has been working here for two years on the 3 to 11 shift. None of the kids have ever respected her because of the way she treats them. She has always let the kids do what they want to do in the units. Miss Maria doesn't care about the kids and the kids can sense that in the way she acts and talks to them. She is just another body on the units and that is enough to make the company happy...

She is a sweet old lady, but she really shouldn't be working with troubled youth, especially if you're just doing it for the money. It isn't that much money anyway so why waste the kid's time. She can make just as much money working at any fast food place...

One of the girls named Jude was having a bad evening so she decided to verbally take it out on Miss Maria. She wasn't responding to Jude's verbal abuse as she called Miss Maria bitches and whores for two straight hours. At 8:00 p.m., Miss Maria finally told Jude that she was going to get her after she went to sleep tonight. Of course she was just playing, but this really upset Jude. She gets even more verbally irate than before. There was only one other girl upstairs with Miss Maria. Her name is Angel and she is in her room religiously listening to music through her earphones. The other kids were downstairs with the other staff doing their nightly chores...

Jude's screams loudly from her room, "I need to go to the bathroom". Miss Maria sarcastically said, "Well go ahead what's stopping you". She puts her head back down to continue reading her Bible. Her precious Bible is something that she reads almost every day and every chance she gets. Jude walked over to where Miss Maria is sitting and angrily said, "Now what bitch". Miss Maria looked up just in time to catch a hard thrown fist across her jaw. She fell out of the chair onto the floor as if she was magnetically pulled downward. Jude jumped on top of her and relentlessly punched her in the head. She then forcefully pulls the wig off Miss Maria's head exposing the short gray hair on her scalp. Jude didn't know she had a wig on; she just wanted to grab a handful of hair and pull it out...

Angel heard all the commotion in spite of the music she was listening to and ran to her door to investigate. She saw Jude standing over Miss Maria with a wig in her hand staring down at her the way a boxer looks down at his opponent after knocking him out. Angel quickly ran out of her room and screamed down the stairs for the other staff to come and help Maria. When Jude heard the screams she quickly went back in her room dropping the wig next to Miss Maria. Angel ran over to Miss Maria and started shaking her shoulder, but there was no response from her. Angel didn't know if Miss Maria was dead or alive...

"Believe in Change"

Chapter 24

"It's all About the Money"

*M*iss Brenda heard Angel loudly screaming for help and frantically ran upstairs. She saw her suspiciously leaning over Miss Maria shaking her shoulders. Not sure what was going on, Miss Brenda ran over like a Linebacker on a football team and violently hit Angel with her shoulder to get her away from Miss Maria. Angel rolls across the floor like a fumbled football, landing about 8 feet away. Miss Brenda hysterically said, "What did you do to her?" She said, "It wasn't me; I was trying to help her. Miss Maria was lying there when I came to my door". Miss Brenda said, "Where is Jude?" Angel said, "She is in her room". At that time Jude came to her door nonchalantly saying, "What do you want? I'm trying to get some rest, could you please keep the noise down". Brenda says, "Do you know what happened to Miss Maria?" Jude says, "She's old as hell, maybe she just died, I don't give a fuck". Then Jude slowly walked back in her room and lays on her bed. Miss Brenda attempts to awaken the motionless body of Miss Maria, but she is still not responding...

Miss Brenda decides that it's time to call 911 because she's not sure what happened to Miss Maria and don't want to take any chances. She needs to stay with Miss Maria so she tells Angel to tell the girls downstairs to come upstairs. Miss Brenda told them to go to their rooms so she could help Miss Maria. All the girls were quietly talking as they paused in the hallway to look at the lifeless body of Miss Maria. They were saying to each other that Miss Maria had a heart attack and she was dead. Most of the girls didn't like Miss Maria, but they seemed truly concerned whether she was dead or not. Miss Brenda saw the bruises on poor Miss Maria's face, but thought that they occurred when she fell to the floor...

Miss Maria starts moving her arms and mumbling, but Miss Brenda couldn't understand anything she was saying. She was attempting to open her eyes, but she couldn't quite get them open. Miss Brenda gets a wet washcloth and put it on Miss Maria's forehead, however this didn't seem to help. Finally the two paramedics arrived and asked Miss Brenda what happened. She told them that she had no idea; she was lying on the floor like that when she found her...

After a few anxious minutes the paramedics had Miss Maria off the floor and sitting on the chair. They must have given her some smelling salts to wake her up. She was awake, but she was continuously complaining about blurred vision and a stiff neck...

One of the paramedics turned to Miss Brenda and said with a serious look on his face, "Someone punched this lady in the head. The lady told us that it was someone named Jude. We are going to take her to the hospital because we believe she has a mild concussion". The paramedics asked Miss Maria if she could walk to the ambulance. She said as her voice began breaking up, "I think so I just need my Bible and I'll be fine". Miss Brenda quickly picked up the Bible and gave it to Miss Maria...

The paramedics help Miss Maria walk because she was staggering from one side of the hall to the other side. She looked like a drunken sailor who had far too many drinks. This was a sad sight to see as Miss Maria staggered down the hallway oblivious to where she was. Some of the girls begin to cry as they watched Miss Maria laboring to stay on her feet...

The supervisor, Miss Ronda showed up just as they were putting Miss Maria in the vehicle. She asked the paramedics was Miss Maria going to be okay. Miss Ronda has a concerned look on her face as she looked back at Miss Maria. He said, "Yes, we think it's just a concussion and hopefully she'll be fine in a couple days". Before Miss Ronda could get another word out of her mouth; they sped off with their lights and sirens making it all so dramatic...

Miss Ronda quickly went in the unit to find out what happened. Miss Brenda angrily said, "Jude violently punched Miss Maria in the head and instantly knocked her unconscious. I found her lying motionless on the floor when I got upstairs"...

Miss Ronda cautiously escorted Jude downstairs to ask her what happened. She wanted to get Jude's point of view before she decided on what to do about the situation. Miss Ronda and Jude sat facing each other on the couch in the TV room. Miss Ronda said calmly, "I know that you hit Miss Maria so don't try to lie to me. I just need to know why you would hit her because she is a sweet old lady with grandkids your age"...

Jude said, "I was scared, Miss Maria said that she was going to kill me after I went to sleep tonight. I had to protect myself, so I got her before she got me". With a surprised look on her face Miss Ronda said, "What exactly did she say to you?" Jude said, "We were arguing and I called her an old bitch, a few times. Then I heard her say, that's okay Jude I'm going to get you while you sleep tonight". Miss Ronda said "Did you really think Miss Maria would do something like that to you?" Jude said, "I don't trust old people, some of them are really crazy and I didn't want to take any chances. People kill other people all the time, just look at the news. I had to do what I had to do and if I had to do it again; then I would do the same thing"...

At the hospital the doctor did an examination and he determined that Miss Maria had a concussion and a sprained neck. Miss Maria was only in the hospital for one day and then they sent her home to rest...

Miss Kate, the (Human Resource Director) called Miss Maria a week later at her house and told her that the company wanted her to work light duty at the Main building. This made Miss Maria very happy to work light duty because she wasn't ready to deal with those girls at the unit yet...

She had a lot of sick time and she was hoping the company would let her use her sick time up instead of coming in to work light duty. If the company allowed her to use sick time then she could stay home until she was feeling better, that would be to humane thing to do...

I met Miss Maria on a Monday in the lunchroom while I was on break. She told me about what happened at the girl's unit and I felt really sorry for her. She seemed like such a nice old lady and didn't deserve to get punched in the face. I told her that she should press charges on Jude for the assault. I also told her if she didn't then it would send the wrong message to the other kids. The other kids on campus would think its okay to assault a staff. This is not a message the staff wants to give to these kids. The kids would be punching the staff all the time if they thought they could get away with it. I explained to Miss Maria what I thought she should do and she agreed...

Miss Maria was surprised to hear that Jude was still on campus and at the unit. I told Miss Maria that as far as I knew nothing had happened to Jude for assaulting her. She was so upset that she stormed out of the lunch room to talk to Miss Kate about it...

Miss Kate greeted Miss Maria with that infamous fake smile of hers. She always had this same smile on her face no matter what staff she was talking to. Everyone knew that the smile wasn't real because it always looked the same. This is a face that Miss Kate has perfected over the many years of lying to the staff...

Miss Maria told her that she wanted to press assault charges on Jude. Miss Kate calmly said, "I understand how you feel, but we want to handle this at the company level for now". Miss Maria angrily said, "How long do you want to keep it like that?" Miss Kate calmly said, "We don't want you to press any charges against Jude until we do more investigating. We don't want you to start a case until we are sure that you are cleared of any wrong-doing"...

Miss Maria loudly said, "So I get punched in the face and this company is not sure if it was my fault? Is that what you are saying?" Miss Kate said, "Jude is definitively saying that you threatened to kill her that day and she was scared, so she had to defend herself. We don't know how true this is, but we can't take any chances right now. So just to be safe, we are going to write this incident up like that for now". Miss Maria said, "So this company isn't going to do anything about me getting assaulted by one of the children?" Miss Kate said, "We don't have enough evidence to pursue this in any other way right now. We need you to bear with us because we don't want to see you lose your job because we moved too fast". Without saying anything else Miss Maria stormed out of the office. She forcefully slammed the door shut behind her leaving Miss Kate with a bemused look on her face...

Miss Maria was almost in tears when I saw her an hour later in the lunchroom. I carefully asked her what was wrong and she told me about her meeting with Miss Kate. I said, "What are you going to do about Jude now since you don't have the support of the company". She humbly said, "I need my job so I guess I'll just be quiet about what happened to me. What else can I do, I need to eat". There was nothing I could say to help her, so I just walked away shaking my head in disbelief. It's pretty sad when a kid can knock the shit out of a staff and there are no consequences for this violence...

These mixed signals that the company always sends to these children always seems to come back and haunt the staff. When the children get confused the first person that they take it out on is the staff because they are right on the unit with them. Most of the kids are here because of confusion and mixed signals in their lives from their parents. This company adds even more negativities to their plates by the way they run this organization. This company is paid a lot of money (a minimum of $200 a day per child) to mess these kids up. Like the boxing promoter, Don King would say "Only in America". He is absolutely right; only

Ron Howard

in America can a company like this be paid $200-$600 a day for not doing anything positive to help a child; what a way to make a living!!!

Two weeks later, Miss Maria was sent back to the girl's unit to work full duty again. Now she has to work with the same child (Jude) who attacked her and this company doesn't give a damn. They are not concerned how that makes Miss Maria feel to have to deal with the child that has got away with assaulting her. They have put her in such an awkward situation that makes it almost impossible for her to do her job properly. However, Maria needs this job so she has to forget about what is right and think about what she has to do to survive financially. This company continues to do what it needs to do to make money and everyone knows that it's all about the money. If Jude leaves then the company will lose $200 a day, but if Miss Maria quits then they don't lose any money. This is simple business math, it's not personal...

The way this company treated Miss Maria hurt her psychologically more than getting physically knocked out by Jude. Mentally, Maria is just a shell of the person she once was and it shows in how she acts and talks. She no longer reads her Bible at work or even at home because she has apparently lost her faith. She doesn't even carry it to work anymore; that's how bad it is for her. It is like she sold her soul to the devil when she kept quiet about what really happened with Jude. How many souls will this company claim in the name of money? This company has been in business for over 100 years and a lot of souls have been destroyed all because of their thirst for money...
"It's all about the money"!! **"Believe in Change"**

169

Chapter 25

"The Irate Parent"

One day while down at the smoke area, one of the staff from another unit named Miss Anne told me an interesting story about Mr. Larry (One of the Three Stooges). She told me that Mr. Larry was under investigation because of what one of the kids was saying. A 16-year-old boy, whose name is Titus said that he and another kid had been giving oral sex to each other in the van during the ride to the YMCA in a nearby town. All of this sexual activities occurred on the weekends when Mr. Larry was working...

This is the story that he surprisingly told the judge when he went to a hearing two weeks ago. Now the whole unit is being investigated for sexual misconduct. Of course Mr. Larry is categorically denying everything as he always does. However Titus is given detailed times and places of the events as they occurred on Mr. Larry shifts...

No one knows exactly why Titus is telling the story because he is on probation for sexually acting out. He will get in trouble for even being near a sexual situation with another child; maybe he just doesn't care anymore...

Several years ago Titus was caught being sexually inappropriate with his 6 year old female cousin. That was 2 years ago when he was 14 years old and he hasn't gotten in trouble since that incident. Maybe he is trying to get even with Mr. Larry for some restraints that were done to him in the past. Maybe one of the other kids persuaded him to tell the story with the hope of getting Mr. Larry fired. Whatever the reason is, he has certainly gotten a lot of people's attention on campus now...

No one on campus is allowed to go to YMCA, especially all the kids from St. Pauls. All of the other units on campus are upset about this, but there is nothing they can do about it. This company does believe in corporal punishment and they will punish everyone for the actions of just one...

Even the Case Manager named Miss Sherry didn't even know Titus was going to tell this story to the judge. She was devastated by his sudden announcement in court. She was pissed and embarrassed to hear everything Titus said to the judge...

Miss Sherry has been at many of these hearings so this was just another day for her at the office. During most of these cases the judge talks to the Case Manager, the Probation Officer, and so on. Titus is usually the last person the judge talks to and this is towards the end of the hearing. The shit really hit the fan when the judge casually asked Titus how things were going at the God's Love Institute. Titus told the judge that everything is fine except for the sex that we have in the van when go to the YMCA on the weekends with Mr. Larry...

All the people in the courtroom looked at each other in shock; they could not believe what Titus just said to the judge. Miss Sherry quickly jumped up and said to Titus, "What are you talking about; you never said anything to me about this". Titus calmly said, "That is because I didn't think you would do anything about it". Titus's mother (Miss Bell) who was also sitting there stood up slowly and said loudly to Titus, "What in the hell are you talking about son?" Titus's Parole Officer who was sitting in the back of the courtroom writing down notes, just put his head down in shame. He simply could not believe what he was hearing from Titus's mouth...

It did not make any sense because Titus knows that he will get in trouble if he's involved in any sexual acting out while he is on probation. Miss Bell was outraged and she shouted across the room to Miss Sherry, "What in the hell is going on at that damn place. These kids aren't being supervised properly!! How in the hell do these kids have time to have oral sex with each other? I want some answers and I want them now". The judge angrily said that he wants some answers also as he called order to courtroom...

The very next day Titus was taken out a God's Love Institute in handcuffs. His Parole officer requested that he be put in a stricter environment for his safety and the other children's safety...

The police came to the school and took Titus out of the classroom in front of everyone. Putting handcuffs on the kid is standard procedure when transporting him/her to another facility. This also gives the other kids something to think about when they see one of their peers being put in handcuffs and put in the back of a police car. The kids on campus aren't sure why the police came to get Titus; all they know is that it was a parole violation...

The police arrested Titus around 11 a.m. and two hours later his mother came to campus to find out what was going on. She went straight to the main building demanding to talk to someone about what happened to her son. The receptionist named Miss Lilly did her best to calm her down. However she wasn't having much luck so she got on the (public announcement system) to call Miss Sherry...

Miss Lilly could smell alcohol and old cigarettes coming from the breath of Titus's mother. Miss Lilly, who is in her early 60s, had a concern for her safety considering the state-of-mind Miss Bell was in. Miss Lilly did not let her into her little office; she talked to her through a small plate glass window that opens and shuts...

Miss Lilly has been working for this company for over 20 years and she is used to hearing unhappy parents. She is like the bartender who listens to the patrons complaining about lives ups and downs. Miss Lilly is a feisty older lady that doesn't take any shit. She also knew that it wasn't her job to fight or argue with any of the parents...

Everyone on the top floor of the main building could hear all the loud noise downstairs. None of them dared to go down and see what was going on for fear of getting involved. This is not the first time they heard an irate parent downstairs in the lobby...

There is no security on campus so anything could happen when an irate parent comes to campus. It is not the staff's job to restrain a parent so what are they supposed to do if violence breaks out. No one knows if this parent has a gun, a knife or some other kind of deadly weapon on them. Miss Bell could have a bomb and there is not one damn thing anyone on campus could do about it except call the local police and hope they get there in time...

After Miss Sherry talked to Miss Lilly, she reluctantly heads down to the main building to hopefully calm the irate Miss Bell down. She was not sure what she's going to say to this poor lady whose son has just been arrested and taken to another facility. Really there is nothing she can say because she has no details on what really happened...

Miss Sherry just found out that Titus was arrested at the school so she is in the dark. Now she has this irate mother at the main building who is going to be asking for answers that she does not have. The reason she don't have answers is because Mr. Derek hasn't taken time to let her know what's going on. He knew that Titus was going to be arrested an hour before it happened, but he failed to let anyone else know about it. This is usually the case with him and most of the staff has gotten used to it. All the staff on campus is sick and tired of dealing with Mr. Derek, but there seems to be nothing they can do about it right now...

On the way down to the main building, Miss Sherry stopped at a few units to see if she could get a staff to go with her to deal with Miss Bell just in case she becomes violent. All of the staff was too busy so she had to go by herself...

While Miss Sherry was walking down to the Main building she was trying to think of things to tell Miss Bell that might bring some resolution to this situation. There was absolutely nothing she could think of that she thought would de-escalate the situation. The only thing that might calm Miss Bell down is probably a good bottle of liquor and maybe a hit of crack cocaine. Miss Sherry thought that if she walked a little slower and took her time to get down to the main building; this would give Miss Bell enough time to settle down...

When Miss Sherry finally arrived she found Miss Bell sitting in the hallway just staring at the wall. Miss Bell looked up and said, "What in the hell took you so long, it's been 30 minutes". Miss Sherry said sarcastically, "I had a few things to do before I could come down here and I'm very sorry. I am here now, what can I do to help you Miss Bell?" She loudly said, "I need to know what happened to my son and I need to know right now". Tears were beginning to form in her eyes as they were nearing the point of overflowing...

Miss Sherry calmly said, "If you come to my office I will explain everything to you". She knew that she couldn't really explain what happened, but she had to say something to this poor lady. Miss Bell said, "You are going to have to wait about five minutes because I need to go smoke a cigarette first". She quickly walked out the door before Miss Sherry can say anything and walked to the smoke area...

On the way back to her office with Miss Bell, Miss Sherry saw Mr. Derek coming out one of the units. When he saw them he suspiciously hurried up and quickly went back in the building. Miss Sherry asked Miss Bell to wait outside for a few minutes while she went in the unit to talk to Mr. Derek...

By the time she gets in the building (a few seconds later) Mr. Derek was already going out the back door. He was walking so fast that it looked like he was late for a very important appointment. Miss Sherry hollered loudly for him, but he acted like he didn't hear her. He didn't even look back when she shouted his name. He couldn't have been more than 15 feet away so she knows that he had to hear her...

Frustrated and angry, Miss Sherry walked back outside to finish what she had to do with Miss Bell. Miss Sherry said, I wanted to get the supervisor of Titus's unit (St. Pauls), but he's just too busy right now. Miss Bell angrily said, "He's too damn busy to talk about my son getting arrested? What can be more important than that? This company gets paid good money to take care of these kids. This is bullshit and I'm going to make sure that (DPW) knows about this". Miss Sherry calmly says, "I understand how you feel, but I don't think you have to go that far. I'm sure we can work this out; we will figure something out" She knew what she just said was a lie, but sometimes a lie is better than the truth when it comes to this company...

The meeting with Mrs. Bell lasted approximately 20 uncomfortable minutes before she stormed out of the office. Everyone on campus could hear her repeatedly cursing Miss Sherry out. She called her every bad name in the book, plus some that weren't in there. There were tears coming from Miss Sherry's eyes by the time Miss Bell left her office. She had never been talked about so badly in her life...

She was furious because the person that should get cursed out is Mr. Derek and he was nowhere to be found. Now she is sitting in her office thinking about how sick and tired she is of doing all the dirty work for Mr. Derek. She decided that she was no longer going to be shit on by Mr. Derek. She is not the only one that is being shit on; he has been shitting on a lot of people at this company. The only person that anyone can figure out that has saved his ass from getting fired has to be Miss Lisa. They have had a relationship for many years and it's going to be hard to separate the two. They have been running this Kingdome for a long time. Either Mr. Derek is going to fall or the company is going to fall. My guess is, "Mr. Derek will fall before the company does"... **"Believe in Change"**

Chapter 26

"*Saying Goodbye to the Stooge*"

It's a month later and Miss Bell is still asking about what God's Love Institute is going to do about Mr. Larry. The company couldn't prove that Mr. Larry did anything wrong, but they had to do something about what happened. Miss Bell has also been coming to campus at least once a week complaining to Miss Sherry and anyone else that would listen to her desperate pleads. She wanted her son back at God's Love Institute because it was more convenient for her to see him...

The place where Titus is at now, Miss Bell can only visit him for two hours a week. Phone calls are $4.50 a minute and that can get very expensive. She can't afford to accept her son's phone calls at home anymore; she simply doesn't have the money for his calls. When Titus was at God's Love Institute, he talked to his mother every day and the calls were free. Now she's on the verge of getting her phone disconnected because the bill is too high. Miss Bell is determined to make life just as miserable for Mr. Larry as it is for her right now...

After constantly getting these complaints from Miss Bell, Mr. Derek wanted Mr. Larry to work the night shift to get him away from St. Pauls. Mr. Derek called Mr. Larry in the office and say, "Miss Bell is making a lot of noise about getting you fired. Maybe if we tell her that you no longer work at St. Pauls she'll go away". Mr. Larry said, "Mr. Derek I need to work on the weekends because I have to baby-sit my kids on the week days". Mr. Derek said in his most authoritative voice, "You have two choices, you can either go to the nightshift or I'm going to have to fire you. What is it going to be Mr. Larry?" He angrily said, "It's fucked up how this company doesn't support its employees. I didn't do anything wrong and I'm getting punished". Mr. Derek said, "You should be happy to have a job right now because I have been covering up for your ass for years. I have got more complaints about you, Mr. Curly and Mr. Moe (The Three Stooges) than any other staff on this campus. I can't do it anymore; I got to cover my ass now". Mr. Larry knew that Mr. Derek was absolutely right, so he let it go...

Finally after several months of waiting, St. Pauls gets another assistant supervisor to everyone's surprise. His name is Mr. Woods. He is a 35 year old African American with an attitude. He has a bald head and only stands about 5 feet tall, weighing about 165 pounds. Most of the kids at St. Pauls could probably beat his ass if they wanted to. Mr. Woods is the first to tell you that it's either his way or the highway. He is going to need this attitude to work for Mr. Derek and the staff at St. Pauls. The company must have finally made Mr. Derek hire another supervisor for the unit. I know he didn't do it on his own because then he would have to share his power. He doesn't like to share power because he wants everyone to run to him when they need something...

Only one of the Three Stooges is still at St. Pauls, so Mr. Woods only has to get rid of one more Stooge and that's Mr. Moe. Once he is out of the unit, Mr. Woods will have a chance of making some positive changes. Mr. Moe is already talking about finding another job because Mr. Woods is making him actually do his job and Mr. Derek is backing him up...

The only thing the Stooge is qualified to do is beat up on kids and steal from them. He shouldn't have a problem getting hired at one of the other organizations in Hopesville that take care of troubled children. He certainly has the qualifications that the other companies seem to be looking for...

Finally God's Love Institute becomes tired of some of the staff coming to work looking like homeless people and implemented a dress code. Everyone had to wear khaki pants and a collared shirt or they will send them home to change. The company only gave the staff two weeks to comply and the company wasn't going to pay for new clothes. There was a lot of bitching and moaning on campus, but the company stayed firm by refusing to pay for the new clothes. The staff at the "School of Education" had to wear uniforms that made them look like doorman at a hotel. They heard a lot of jokes about their uniforms, but they took it in stride...

The company had decided to take on a more professional look, but they still had the same unprofessional staff working here. You can put a suit on a clown, but underneath the suit there is still a clown. At least God's Love Institute has professional looking clowns now so they can still fool the public. This is the first sign of improvement that I have seen from God's Love Institute since I started working here. I guess my prayers are working. Believe in the power of prayer...

After a few weeks on night shift Mr. Larry gets child-lined again for slapping Jude. She is the same kid who attacked Miss Maria and didn't get in any trouble for doing it. She was verbally acting out and Larry went to see if he could calm her down. Jude was threatening to assault Miss Brenda...

Jude really didn't want to jump on Miss Brenda because she knew that she would probably get a good ass beating from her. All the kids knew that Miss Brenda did not take any shit. All the staff on campus has been waiting for an excuse to restrain Jude every since she punched Miss Maria in the face...

When Jude saw Mr. Larry she quickly went back in her room. It was 12:30 a.m. and Jude had the whole unit awake because of all the noise she was making. There were several additional staff there, but no one was having any success in calming Jude down. Mr. Larry said loudly, "Listen up, I'm here now and you little motherfuckers better settle down. Anyone who knows me knows that I don't fuck around". Jude quickly came to her doorway and said at the top of her lungs, "Shut the fuck up, I don't give a damn about you"...

The other kids started laughing loudly at her comment. Mr. Larry's face turned beet red with embarrassment and he angrily said, "You better take your ass back in that room while you can". Jude stepped out in the hallway and said, "Shut up you white ass faggot". She went in her room after she spit towards were Mr. Larry was standing...

Mr. Larry quickly ran down to Jude's room and walked slowly and cautiously inside. She said loudly, "Get the fuck out of my room bitch". Mr. Larry said, "You better calm down before I hurt you". She said, "I'm not scared of you. I'll fuck you up just like I've fucked up that old ass Miss Maria". The next noise that came out of Jude's room was a sound of a man's open hand going across her face. The sound could be heard by everyone upstairs, it was like it was in stereo. Silence filled the hallways as everyone listened for the next sound to come from Jude's room. After Jude got over the shock of getting the shit slapped out of her (which was a few seconds later) she screamed hysterically saying, "He hit me, that motherfucker hit me"...

Mr. Larry smiled at Jude and calmly walked out of the room. She knew better than to try to hit him back, she wasn't that crazy. All the kids on campus knew how much Mr. Larry enjoyed restraining kids and she wasn't going to give him any enjoyment today...

He calmly sat down in a chair in a hallway as if nothing happened. Everything he did seemed so mechanical; it was like he was a machine without soul. Miss Brenda didn't ask Mr. Larry what happened because she didn't want to get involved. She walked down to Jude's room to check on her because it sounded like he hit her real hard. She found Jude lying across her bed; she was holding her face while crying into her pillow like a little baby...

Miss Brenda didn't really like Jude, but she was saddened to see her quietly crying on her bed. Jude didn't want any of her peers to hear or see her crying because that would mess up our reputation of being tough. Miss Brenda knew that some of the kids can be assholes, but that doesn't give any of the staff the right to slap them like Mr. Larry did...

Miss Brenda doesn't know Mr. Larry that well, she only knows of his reputation for beating on the kids. She always made sure that she never had to work with him because she knew how he was. Miss Brenda does everything by the book and she doesn't play when it comes to hurting the kids. She is one of the very few employees that Janet and I respect at God's Love Institute...

She knows about him, Mr. Moe and Mr. Curly and the way they had been treating kids for years. Jude showed Miss Brenda her face where Mr. Larry viciously hit her. It looked like Jude took a red marker pen and colored the outline of Mr. Larry's hand on her face. He must have hit her real hard because the police could take fingerprints off of Jude's face if they needed some evidence to prove this case...

When Mr. Larry came to the unit tonight, it was like a tornado had dropped from the clouds and caused mass destruction, then disappeared back in the sky. I believe he is a freak of nature because he has something missing from inside his brain that makes him not care about hurting children. A normal person has feelings for these children that have been separated from their families with very little chance of ever having a typical childhood. Creatures like Mr. Larry should never be near these children or any child...

Mr. Mott, the new supervisor of the girls units was very upset when he heard about what Mr. Larry did. Miss Ronda, who used to be the supervisor of the girls units, got fed up with the bullshit at God's Love Institute and quit about a month ago and Mr. Mott took over...

Mr. Larry denied slapping Jude or even touching her, but there was too much evidence against him. How did he expect to get out of this one especially since there were fingerprints across the girl's face? Every since the incident with Titus at St. Pauls, the company has been waiting for any reason to finally get rid of

Mr. Larry. Mr. Mott told Mr. Larry that he was child-lined and not allowed in the girls units until the investigation was completed. He could tell by the tone in Mr. Mott's voice that it was just a matter of time before the company would fire him. It wasn't long before Mr. Larry started putting in his applications for other jobs outside of God's Love Institute...

Two weeks later after finding another job he quit without notice. He didn't give the company the pleasure of firing him because he knew they were going to put the child abuse case on his record. He didn't want that on his record just in case he wanted to work with kids again...

He found a job as a "Water meter reader" in the town of Hopesville, which sounds appropriate for him. He is still going to be out in the neighborhoods where children are and I'm sure he will find an excuse to jump on some poor kid in some unsuspecting neighborhood...

The company was so happy to get rid of Mr. Larry that they dropped all charges against him on the child-line. It just suddenly got swept underneath the table like all of the other ones. They told all the concerned parties that the company terminated him for slapping Jude, which was a lie because he quit. Mr. Larry was smart enough to quit while he was still ahead. He still has his perfect record of never losing a child-line case; I am sure that makes him proud...

The problem that I have with this whole situation is that he is still capable of working with kids again. He doesn't have a child abuse record or conviction to stop him. This is not good for the children of the world or our society. Here is my message to Mr. Larry, Mr. Moe and Mr. Curly; "You do not want to go to prison after being convicted of child abuse because you will not be happy with what the inmates will do to you...
"Believe in Change"

Chapter 27

"The Banned Book"

*S*hortly after Mr. Larry quit, to everyone's surprise Mr. Moe put in his two week notice. He no longer had the psychological support of the other two stooges and I guess that bothered him. He was so used to working with Curly and Larry and he felt lost without them to cheer him on. When they worked together, they seem to draw and absorb negative energy from each other. This energy that they created gave them their false sense of power over to children. Now that the team is broken up, (Larry, Curly and Moe) they don't feel like they can survive in this environment with troubled youth. This is just my theory on their work relationship. It wasn't long before Mr. Moe finds a job working in a factory. I am not sure what kind work he does in the factory, but at least he's away from children...

Mr. Stan (Moe's best friend) also tries to find another job; because he is African American with no college degree I believe it's the reason he had no success. Mr. Larry and Mr. Moe have no college background, but they are White males and that's all they needed to find other employment in Hopesville...

When I first met Mr. Stan, I explained to him the importance of getting a college degree, but he didn't listen to me. He was too busy working overtime so that his son could have a better life. He is starting to understand now since he has been trying to find a job in Hopesville. Unless Mr. Stan does something different, it looks like he's going to be stuck at God's Love Institute for a long time or until he gets fired. At least he is not like the Three Stooges so that's a blessing if he does have to stay at God's Love Institute...

After four years of writing in my spare time, my book is done and ready to sale. There is a buzz and excitement in the air because I have told everyone about my book and they have been waiting patiently for the release of it. The book documents my past discrepancies as a young boy growing up in poverty and crime...

A lot of the kids that I work with are in similar situations and don't believe that they can change. I wanted to let the kids know that I am living proof that they can change their situation in a positive direction. My book wasn't written to make money, it was written because I wanted more people to know where I was in life and where I'm at right now. Hopefully I can inspire someone to attempt to make their life better. If I can inspire one person, then I will consider my book a success...

Almost all the staff on campus purchased a copy of the book when it was released, except a few haters. Even God's Love Institute was talking about ordering copies for the school classrooms. Even the Sister said that she wanted to buy a copy of the book. The book is doing well; it is at Borders, Amazon and Barnes & Noble right now. Everything is going great; I am amazed at how well the book is doing...

A month later, everything changed at God's Love Institute. All of a sudden people in management weren't speaking to me anymore. Now when they see me walking down the hall they find an excuse to walk in another direction. These actions left me with an uncomfortable feeling, a feeling that's hard to describe...

Miss Kate, the (Director of Human Resources) called me in her office one morning at 9 a.m. I wasn't sure what she wanted to see me about, but I had a feeling that it was nothing good. I knew that she cheerfully told me a few weeks ago that she wanted to purchase a copy of my book, so maybe that's it...

She was very cordial as usual when she started to talk to me in her office. She started the conversation off by asking me how I was feeling and how my family was was doing. Then she said with a serious look on her face, "You are not allowed to solicit your book on campus anymore because of company policies. Don't get me wrong, we are very proud that you wrote a book. We have 700 employees and if we do that for you, than we will have to do it for them also". I said calmly, "I haven't been soliciting my book on campus. People have been coming to me and requesting copies". She said, "From now on you will have to sell the book off campus". I said, "What if the Sister asks for a copy of the book?" She said, "I don't think she will be asking for one now". I sarcastically said, "Okay, whatever this company needs; I wouldn't want to do anything to lower the standards of this great company". I smiled as I exited out of her office...

The conversation with Miss Kate took me by surprise because I didn't believe those words would actually come out of her mouth. I knew something was going on, but I didn't expect the company to outright say my book is banned on campus. This company is constantly amazing me with their bullshit, boy are they good...

I found out a few days later that Mr. Derek was the one who went to the Sister and told her about the contents of my book. He told her about the sex, drugs and crime that were strategically spread throughout the pages of my book. She couldn't believe that this company has someone with my past working here with their children...

The Sister set up a meeting with all the Supervisors and Directors to discuss the sale of my book. At the meeting, she explained to everyone that the sale of my books had to stop on campus immediately. She wanted to make sure that God's Love Institute was not associated with that book in any way...

Mr. Derek didn't even buy the book he read, he borrowed it from one of the staff named Mr. Terry. I don't know if he was told by management to read the book or if he came up with the idea on his own. I believe he was trying some way to get back at me for abdicating from the position of supervisor...

The first real sign of my book being banned on campus was when I went to get the money that Miss Sherry the (Supervisor of Case-Managers) owed me for a book. She is a 36-year-old female who has been working for this company for five years. She is a very attractive African-American with a Masters degree in psychology. I met her when I first started working at God's Love Institute three years ago. She is a divorced mother with three young kids. She seems to have a bright future here because she knows all the right people. When my book was released, she was the first one in line to get a copy. She just didn't have any money at the time so I took her credit...

One day I went to Miss Sherry's office, which is right across the hall from Miss Lisa's office (The Director of Residential Living). Miss Lisa and Miss Sherry are very good friends. I can always get some good gossip from Miss Sherry because of the relationship that she has with Miss Lisa. Her office is not located at the main building; it is right on campus on the bottom floor of one of the units named Zachariah Hall...

When I sat down in her office she gets up and closed the door behind me. She usually does that when she has some good gossip to tell me, but today she has a serious look on her face. It was like she has some bad news, but wasn't sure how to say it to me. I smiled and said, "What's wrong, did you get fired or something?" She quietly said, "I'm not allowed to buy your book on campus now so I need to get your home address. I can mail you the money that I owe you. I said, "You already have the book so who's going to know if you hand me $15 right now? No one can see through the door. At least I don't think they can". She said, "I just don't want to take any chances with Miss Lisa's office being across the hall". I said in a condescending voice, "Damn they really got you scare don't they? What did this company do to you? Did they threaten to fire you if you purchase a book from me?" She just stood there with a puzzled look on her face with no response to my question. I can see the fear and embarrassment written all over her face so I decided it was time to leave...

"Children on Layaway, it's all about the Money$$$"

It was sad to see that kind of fear on the face of the educated black woman. She made me think of a "House-Nigger" that was not allowed to talk to one of the field slaves. Miss Sherry should be supporting her positive black brothers, but instead she is letting the white man control her feelings. I can understand her being scared to lose her job, but where is her pride as a black woman. Why do some of my black brothers and sisters think that education will change their skin color?

I am still not going to quit selling my book on campus; if someone wants a copy I'll just go to the trunk of my car and get it for them. My book is unofficially banned on campus; no one even mentions the name of the book anymore. All of the kids on campus know about the book and they always flocked to me to ask me about it. The kids are very impressed that I wrote a book about my past and that is more important than what the company thinks about me...

Now many of the kids on campus are talking about writing their own book. I encourage each kid that I speak to about my book because these kids need positive encouragement. I would love to see them all be writers someday because I know they all have great stories to tell. I am happy that I'm having a positive influence on the kids because of the book. I really don't give a damn what this company thinks about this ex-drug dealer and pimp. However I do care what the kids think about me and that's what counts...

Since the release of my book, I had four book signings at the Borders stores in Hopesville. Out of all the people at God's Love Institute, only one person came to one of my book signings. I was surprised when I saw Miss Peaches standing in line to get a signed copy of my book. She is a middle-aged white lady, who I met during an interview when I applied for another position at God's Love Institute. She is a very nice lady who has been working for this company for over 20 years. She works at a different branch of God's Love Institute that is on the other side of town. She doesn't have to deal with Residential Living; maybe that is why she is such a nice person...

Not one African-American staff came out to support my book. I don't know if they are scared that the company will find out or if they are just haters. I would like to think that this company doesn't have that kind of power over my black brothers and sisters. It would make me feel better to know that they are just haters...

One day, Miss Kate calls me in our office and tells me that she has light duty work at "Alternative Education". This is a building located about a block away from the campus. I believe that the company just didn't want me in the main building anymore because of my outspoken ways and my book. I'm sure they were worried about what I might say if a visitor or a Board Member asked me what I thought about this organization. Anyone that knows me knows that I'm going to tell them exactly what's on my mind. I have been telling anyone who will listen about the problems that I have encountered at this organization, but no one is listening. I guess God's Love Institute figures if I am out of sight, then I will be out of mind...

The company knows that there is nothing for me to do at Alternative Education. I sit there for eight hours a day and write; I guess you could say that God's Love Institute is helping me finish this book about them...

Alternative Education is a part of God's Love Institute where the kids can come and learn carpentry, basic electric and basic plumbing skills. This is one of the better programs here because this gives the kids something to really fall back on out in the real world. All the kids that come here aren't going to be college material. I have been here for three years and Alternative Education is the only program that makes sense for most of the kids that come here. It is a good program, but it wouldn't be anything if it didn't have a good caring staff to teach it. It is the good staff and supervision that make this program work...

"Believe in Change"

Chapter 28

"Stop dating my Mom"

One thing that I can say about God's Love Institute is that they will hire almost anyone to work in residential living. Sexual preference is not important to this company as long as each shift is full. This career field doesn't pay much money so God's Love Institute doesn't expect to hire the "cream of the crop". There is no incentive for the company to pay more money when they can get away with hiring almost anyone. God's Love Institute makes the same amount of money per child whether or not the new employee has a degree or not. The company has hired employees who have weighed as much as 400 pounds and been as little as 100 pounds to work with these children. The company doesn't care how tall you are or how short you are just as long as they got a body on the unit, then they are happy. There is one thing that I haven't seen yet and that is the company hire any gay men. I'm not sure if they have been discriminating or if no gay men have tried to get a job here yet...

Recently the company did hire a gay woman named Miss Samantha to work in a girl's units. The name of a unit is called St. Monica and it's a residential therapeutic facility where all the kids have some kind of mental health issues. Miss Samantha and has no formal education that involves working with mental health problems. She is outwardly gay and not ashamed to say it to the staff or the kids. She is about 5 foot six, weighs about 220 pounds and dresses just like a man. She has piercings in her ears and her eyebrows. There is nothing that is feminine about her. She looks and acts tougher than the majority of the males who work here. She is very outspoken and whatever's on her mind she makes sure that the staff and the kids know about it. The kids appreciate how outspoken she is, but some of the staff do not like it. She has only been here a few months and has been in several verbal altercations with other staff about how to run the unit. This is what she tells the other staff, "I am here for the kids and I don't give a damn how you feel about me"...

A few months later, one of the girls at St. Monica was talking to their mother on the phone. This routine is something most of the kids do every night and she surprisingly hears a familiar voice in the background. The girl's name is Ruth, a 14-year-old African-American who has been in residential living off and on for most of her young life. Her mother named Lenore is a 30-year-old crack addict who has no idea who Ruth's father is...

Ruth calls her mother every day from the unit because she enjoys talking to her mother in spite of the unfortunate circumstances. For now, the only time she will see her mother is at the family therapy session; which is always on campus. Ruth's mother just can't seem to be able to kick the crack addiction long enough to get her back home. Ruth has become strangely accustomed to her mother letting her down, but she still has a special love that only a child would understand...

After hearing that familiar voice a few more times she curiously asked her mother who it is. Ruth calmly said, "Mom who is that I hear in the background?" Her mother proudly said, "Oh that's my new girlfriend named, Samantha. We have been dating for a few weeks now, but this is the first time that she has come to visit me". Ruth anxiously said, "What does she look like because she sounds like someone who works here from 7 a.m. to 3 p.m. Monday through Friday. Her mother describes what her new girlfriend looks like as Ruth quietly listens. Ruth said, "Where does she work mom?" She said, "I'm not sure, let me ask Samantha". Her mother puts the phone down and shouts across the room; "Samantha, where do you work at?" Ruth listened closely as the familiar voice say very clearly; "I work at God's

Love Institute". Those were the last words that Ruth wanted to hear. Those words burned in her ears like hot flaming coals...

Her mother told her a year ago that she was dating women and didn't want anything else to do with men anymore. Ruth didn't care if she dated men or women, she just wanted to go home and live with her mother again...

Ruth angrily said, "Mom that's the same Miss Samantha who works on my unit. This is bullshit and I'm not going to put up with it. It will be so embarrassing if the other kids find out that Miss Samantha is dating my mom". Before her mother could get another word out of her mouth, Ruth hung the phone up and ran back to her room...

Ruth's mother made several attempts to talk to her again, but Ruth wouldn't get on the phone. The staff tried to find out what was wrong with Ruth, but she wouldn't tell them anything. For the next three hours Ruth laid across her bed and cried. She wouldn't even talk to her roommate, who wasn't sure what was going on with her...

Later on that night when Miss Janet came to work, Ruth was still quietly lying on her bed. When Miss Janet was done during her bed checks and heading back to where she would be sitting for the rest of the night she heard a whispering voice coming from Ruth's room. Miss Janet said in a quiet but firm voice, "Who is that standing in the doorway down there? Everyone is supposed to be in bed sleeping". Ruth anxiously said, "Miss Janet can I please talk to you, it's very important". Miss Janet could hear the seriousness in Ruth's voice, but the staff didn't mention anything about Ruth having any problems today. Miss Janet has a rapport with all the girls; they all know that they can come to her about any problem and she is willing to sit down and listen. That is the kind of person she is and the kind of person all staff should try to emulate...

Miss Janet said, "Is this something that can wait until tomorrow morning?" With a sad look on her face Ruth said, "I have been holding this inside for hours; I really need to talk to someone right now. Please Miss Janet you simply got to let me talk to you about what's on my mind". Miss Janet said, "Come on and let's go downstairs so we can talk privately in the office"...

Janet told Miss Gadget that she would be right back as soon as you find out what's wrong with Ruth. After Janet made sure that Ruth was comfortable in the office she then asked her what was on her mind. Ruth hesitated for a few seconds as if she was gathering her thoughts before speaking. With a desperate look on her face she said, "Miss Janet I have a serious problem and I don't know who to talk to about it. I can't talk to the other staff because I don't trust them. You are the only one that I've been able to talk to since I've been here". Miss Janet said, "I'm glad that you feel that way because that is how I want you to feel about me. So why don't you tell me what's on your mind and let's see if I can help you". A sigh of relief came from Ruth as she sank deeper into her chair. Finally she has someone that she trusts and can confide in. It is so important for a child to have a loving and caring adult that they can put their trust into...

With a newfound confidence Ruth said, "My mother turned gay about a year ago and I had to learn to deal with that. It didn't really matter to me because I wasn't living at home anyway. Since I don't have any brothers or sisters, I didn't have to worry about them getting mixed up in my mother's craziness. None of the kids on the unit know about my mother being gay so I didn't have to worry about them teasing me. They already know that she is a "Crackhead" because I have told all of them. I can live with the kids knowing that my mom is a drug addict, but I don't think I can live with them knowing that she is gay and dating one of the staff that works here". This statement shocked Miss Janet because in her wildest dreams she did not expect to hear this come from this child's mouth. Complete silence filled the air as Janet just stared across at Ruth trying to gather her thoughts before she responded to the statement that this poor child just made...

With a sudden urgency in her voice Miss Janet said, "What staff is your mother supposed to be dating?" Ruth said, "It is Miss Samantha on daylight. Tonight when I was talking to my mom on the phone I heard her voice in the background and I asked my mom who it was. That is when she told me that it was Miss Samantha and they have been dating for a couple weeks now". Miss Janet said, "Are you sure that it is the same Miss Samantha who works at this unit?" Ruth said, Miss Samantha told her tonight while I was listening where she worked at. I heard her very clearly, I know what I heard and I know whose voice I heard. I need to know what I can do about it". Miss Janet told her to wait in the office because she needed to make a private phone call. Actually Miss Janet wasn't sure what to do so she wanted to talk to me first. She knew that she could get some good advice from me (Mr. Renaldo) because I used to be a supervisor...

I was shocked to hear the story but I gave her the best advice that I could. I told her to leave a message with Mr. Derek about the situation and be sure to let him know how upset the child is about it. I also told her to fill out an incident report just to cover her back...

Miss Janet went back in the office to tell Ruth what the game plan was. Ruth was sitting there waiting patiently and a smile came across the face as she walked in. Miss Janet calmly said, "I left a message with Miss Samantha's supervisor Mr. Derek and I'm sure that he is going to take care of this right away". With a concerned look on her face Ruth said, "But what if he doesn't. I can't be in the same unit as someone that is dating my mom. Something just isn't right about that. It doesn't matter if she's a staff or not she shouldn't be dating my mom". Miss Janet said, "You are absolutely right and I promise you this, I will do everything that I can to make sure this stops". Ruth stood up with tears beginning to fall down her face and said, "Thank you Miss Janet, I don't know what I would do without you to talk to". Miss Janet stood up and gave Ruth a hug then whispered in her ear, "You are welcome, anytime I can help you out, I will always be there for you...

Miss Samantha got a call before she left for work at 6 a.m. from Mr. Derek. He told her not to go to the unit because he has something very important to talk to her about. He asked her to meet him at his office at 9 a.m. Miss Samantha had a suspicion about what he wanted to talk about, but she wasn't sure how he was planning on resolving it. She really didn't see anything wrong with dating one of the kid's mothers. There was nothing in the employee handbook that said she couldn't date one of the kid's parents...

This is the first time that Mr. Derek ever had to resolve a problem like this and he has been working here for long time. I don't know anyone in their right mind who would want a date a known Crackhead like Ruth's mother. What does that say about Miss Samantha and what does that say about the company that hires these kinds of people. I would certainly like to sit in on this meeting between Mr. Derek and Miss Samantha; it should be pretty interesting...

Ruth was happy when she woke up in the morning and didn't see Miss Samantha on the unit. Miss Janet was also happy when Miss Samantha didn't show up for work because she wasn't sure how Ruth was going to react when she saw her. Because she didn't show up for work, Miss Janet had to stay late and help the girls get ready for school. This is one time she didn't mind working overtime because the staff didn't show up on time...

Ruth gave Miss Janet another big hug as she was leaving the building to go to school. When she was heading out the door she turned around and said, "Thanks Miss Janet you are my angel". None of the other staff knew what was going on with Miss Samantha and Ruth. Miss Janet wasn't planning on saying anything because she knows how the staff loves to gossip on campus...

"Children on Layaway, it's all about the Money$$$"

Mr. Derek met Miss Samantha at 9 a.m. exactly and they walked into his office together. He said, "I heard some disturbing news last night about you dating one of the children's parents. I need to ask you whether or not this is true. She arrogantly said, "We have been dating for a few weeks now, but I don't know why that is any of the company's business. Who I date is my business"!! Mr. Derek calmly said, "Normally it is your business, but when affects one of the children that live here on campus then it becomes our business. I am trying to be nice so you need to change your attitude". She said, "I don't have an attitude; I just don't like people in my business. There is nothing in the employee handbook that says that I cannot date a parent of one of the children". Mr. Derek said, "I know there's nothing in the employee handbook about a situation like this, but I'm not going to let you work in the same unit with the child. You have two options; the first one is that you can go work at St. Pauls or you can pack your bags and go home. Which one is it going to be Miss Samantha?"

Miss Samantha thought about it for a few seconds and said, I guess I have no choice because I need my job. I still don't think it's fair that this company gets to determine who their employees date. When do you want me to start working at St. Pauls?" Mr. Derek said, "You can start as soon as you leave this office and if I hear about you dating any of the boys parents I'm going to fire you right on the spot. Whether you know it or not, I am giving you break so you should be thankful. There is one more thing; I do not want you to mention anything about you dating Ruth's mother or any other parents of these children. That will not be the kind of news that will help you keep your job at God's Love Institute". Miss Samantha walked out of Mr. Derek's office slamming the door behind her...

St. Pauls is an all boys unit where the kids ranging in age from 12 to 18. No one can be sure how the boys will react to having a gay female working on the unit, but it is probably safer

194

for Miss Samantha to be at St. Pauls with boys than it would be for her to be around a lot of young girls...

I'm not sure why the company hired Miss Samantha considering how she'd looked and acted when they interviewed her. What would make them think that she would be good working with any kids; especially the already confused children that are in residential living? God only knows what's going to happen at St. Pauls when Miss Samantha gets there with her attitude. With the help of God there is always a chance that everything will be all right and the boys will get along fine with her... **"Believe in Change"**

Chapter 29

"Where's our vehicle"

One night at 3 a.m. while the staff at one of the boys units (Zechariah Hall) was sleeping, three of the kids stole one of the vehicles. The office was left open and they just walked in and stole the keys. That is just how simple it was, especially since the staff was all asleep as usual. No one knew the boys were gone until the morning staff came to work the next day. The morning staff didn't even find out until 10 o'clock in the morning because when the morning staff got to work they went to sleep for a few hours...

Normal procedure is for every shift to check the rooms to see if all the kids are there, but this is rarely done. Actually one of the kids had to wake the staff up to let them know that three of the boys were gone...

The staff frantically searched all over campus, but the boys were nowhere to be found so they notified the supervisor and the local police. It wasn't until one o'clock that afternoon that they realize one of the vehicles was gone. After confirming that no other unit had their vehicle, the staff had to call the police and the supervisor again to let them know that the vehicle was also stolen by the three boys...

What had seemed like a simple runaway had now turned into a terrible nightmare for God's Love Institute. The company expected to get a phone call from the police saying that their vehicle was wrecked, but they didn't get a call or hear anything the whole weekend...

This could possibly turn into the company's worst nightmare if these boys kill someone with their vehicle. This kind of stuff would never happen if the staff would just simply do their jobs or if the company made sure that proper procedure was being followed by the staff...

The local and city police were on the lookout for the boys all weekend and had no luck in finding the boys or the stolen vehicle. It was like they disappeared into thin air...

After being gone since Friday night, all three boys calmly walked back on campus as if nothing happened. They showed up on Monday afternoon around 1 p.m. looking like they haven't seen a toothbrush or bar of soap all weekend. The boys walked up to the main building and told Miss Lilly (The receptionist) who they were. All she did was shake her head in disappointment and called their unit to come and get them. The boys were laughing and joking in the lobby like they didn't have a care in the world. Miss Lilly said, "I hope you had fun this weekend because you have pissed off a lot of people on campus". One of the boys looked at her and said, "We had a ball, we are going to have to do this again sometime"...

The company knew that none of the boys had a driver's license or even a permit because the ages of the boys are 13, 14 and 15 years old. That doesn't mean that one of them didn't have an illegal license that he had used...

The first thing the staff asked the boys was where the vehicle was. Almost simultaneously the boys said, "What vehicle are you talking about? We don't have a license to drive a vehicle; what are you talking about?" Staff angrily said, "We know you stole the damn vehicle, we just want to know where it is. If you don't tell us where it's at, then you're going to be arrested for auto theft and the police are going to lock your ass up for long time". One of the boys said, "We did not steal a vehicle and you can't pin that shit on us. What proof do you have that we stole a vehicle?" Frustrated the staff said, "All three of you motherfuckers go to your rooms because I'm tired of talking to you. Mr. Derek is on his way to campus and I hope you fucking idiots don't tell him the same dumb-ass story"...

Later on Mr. Derek came to campus and questioned the boys separately, but had no luck finding out where the vehicle was. He told the staff to take away all the boy's privileges until further notice. He thought that would encourage the boys to tell the truth. After two weeks of all the boys being put on lockdown, their story still was to same...

Now the whole campus is talking about the stolen vehicle and how no one can find out where it is. The three boys had the staff and God's Love Institute looking like hopeless fools. The staff really wanted to beat the shit out of the boys, but they knew that everybody was watching their every move since the incident...

Even the kids on campus were surprised to hear that none of the staff had beaten the boys up yet. It was very fortunate for the boys that management was keeping an eye on them because staff wanted to beat them very bad. Staff knew that if they did anything to the boys it would get too much attention right now. This situation is hard for the staff because they are used to beating on the kids and not worrying about management giving a damn. Hopefully for the staff this storm will pass and they can go back to beating the kids like they normally do...

The staff wanted to have the boys put in jail for car theft, but they had no proof they stole the vehicle. The other kids on campus began to admire the fact that the boys would not tell where the vehicle was. The three boys were beginning to be treated by the other kids like kings on campus instead of criminals...

This was really pissing off the staff; it was hard for the staff to watch these boys laughing and joking with the other kids like they knew for sure nothing was going to happen to them. The company simply can't just sit back while these three criminals become heroes on campus. This is sending a bad message to the staff and to the kids. Everyone on campus knows that the three boys stole the vehicle and yet they have received no consequences for this crime other than lost of privileges. I don't know what's taken the company so long to do something, but I know they need to do something fast...

The company's next strategy is to put all three boys in different units on campus. They wanted to separate them to see if they would be able to create a weakness in their story. I don't know where they are getting these ideas from, but it is obvious to me that it's not coming from anyone who knows anything about kids who grow up in the streets...

Now a whole month has passed since the incident and the company is still unable to find out where their vehicle is. The company desperately wants to fire the person who was working the night the vehicle was stolen, but they haven't been able to recruit any new employees yet. The Sister is very disappointed and angry and the supervisors can sense some pending doom coming their way. Mr. Derek met with the boys separately one last time to try to persuade them with gifts and money to tell him where the vehicle is. All the boys literally laughed in his face in spite of getting offered hundreds of dollars in gifts and money. No one knows if the boys are scared to say something or if they are just that tough...

Over 30 days have passed and now the police aren't actively looking for the vehicle anymore. It is beginning to look like the vehicle is never going to show up again. This is really looking bad for the company; they have three boys on campus who are known car thieves and nothing has happened to them yet. What message is being sent to the other children? What message is being sent to the boys who stole the vehicle? The message is that kids can steal a vehicle and nothing will happen to the child...

Two months after the vehicle was stolen the police came to campus to talk to the boys again. The boys were a little nervous because they weren't absolutely sure what the police wanted to talk to them about. The police spoke to the boys individually after they explained to God's Love Institute what was going on. They told God's Love Institute that the stolen vehicle was used to rob a bank and the driver and the three passengers were killed by gunfire from the police. The driver of the van, a 17-year-old teenager is the cousin of one of the boys who stole the van two months ago. The Sister is devastated by this news and paces back and forth speechless. The police told the Sister that all the boys that were killed were known members of the gang called "bloods". The youngest kid was 13 years old and the oldest was 17 years of age...

They are all African-American youth with similar backgrounds as the kids in residential living on campus. The police didn't find out anything from the three boys in spite of an intense interrogation from them. The police questioned the boys for hours on campus, but the boys definitively denied having anything to do with stealing the vehicle from the unit...

The Sister asked the police to do her a favor and keep God's Love Institute out of the newspapers. It would be very embarrassing to have God's Love Institute linked to this type of criminal activity, especially since the lives of four teenagers was taken by the police in one of God's Love Institute's vehicles...

For over a hundred years, God's Love Institute has had a reputation of saving young lives; this incident would be an extreme blemish on their record. The police agreed that it would do no good by linking God's Love Institute to the van so they promise the Sister that there would be no mention of the van being stolen from God's Love Institute...

The Sister felt like a great weight had been lifted off her shoulders and now she can see the light at the end of this tunnel of doom. The company is going to have to do something very fast to get rid of all connections to this mess...

The company decides that it would be in their best interests to send the boys somewhere else. The sooner the Sister gets the boys off campus, the sooner she will be able to sleep at night again. Three days after the police had come to campus; all the boys had been sent to different residential living throughout the State of Pennsylvania. The company didn't even call the parents until the boys were in transit to their new residential living. The staff that has waited so patiently to get a chance to abuse the kids didn't even have time to get that satisfaction. They got the kids off campus so fast it was like they had a contagious disease. None of the boys put up any resistance to leaving God's Love Institute. They were more than happy to get away from the staff that had been biding their time so that they can get their revenge for all the trouble that they caused them...

God's Love Institute had no problem finding placement for all three of the boys. As a matter of fact it is the easiest thing in the world to take your child to one of these companies and leave them for minimum of 90 days. I personally call it "Children on Layaway" because it is set up similar to the layaways at the retail stores in the United States. Once the parent had filled out the necessary paperwork, they have 90 days to get themselves together mentally and physically or the child will be there for an additional 90 days. Metaphorically the children are put on shelves or hangers like clothing until the parent comes back to get them. Only in rare occasions do these parents actually come back to get their children. Usually the company will have them until their 18th birthday and sometimes longer. The children are literally on layaway. Now you understand why this book is titled "Children on Layaway"...

"Believe in Change"

Chapter 30

"Sharing the Aids Virus"

Aids has been around for awhile now so it is expected that some kids at God's Love Institute will have the HIV virus or full-blown AIDS. Because of confidentiality, the company is not allowed to share this information with the staff. Usually the staff can determine who has AIDS by the medication that the kid has to take every day...

In orientation when an employee is first hired; they are warned about the possibility of any kid having the AIDS virus. Universal precautions are encouraged at all times when working with the children. I personally keep a pair of rubber gloves in my back pocket during every shift. Staff is told to always use rubber gloves if any of the children are bleeding. There is hardly a day that goes by when someone isn't bleeding on the units. Every day there is a restraint or a fight or the kids are just falling down while playing. The kids should not be the only concern when it comes to the AIDS virus because no one knows what contagious diseases the staff has. They also could have a multitude of diseases that they don't want anyone to know about. It is not unusual for a staff to be bleeding after or during a restraint of a child. No matter who it is, we all have to use caution when blood is involved...

In spite of the fact that the company is the only one who's supposed to know which child has AIDS, many of the staff openly talks about the children who have AIDS on this campus. Mr. Larry is the main culprit in spreading this personal news on this campus. He is legendary for running his big mouth. I had only been on the job a few days before he told me which kids had AIDS. Here are his exact words, "There are two kids on this campus who have AIDS and that is Abraham and Corinthian. I don't care what they are doing, I won't fucking touch them for no reason at all. They can be banging their heads off the wall until their brains are spilling out and I still won't go near them. They could be sitting there cutting their wrists and I still will refuse to help them. Those fucking kids with AIDS shouldn't be in this place anyway. The staff shouldn't have to worry about getting that damn AIDS. This company doesn't pay enough money for staff to worry about this shit"…

When he told me about this we were sitting in the hallway of St. Pauls where all the other kids could hear him talking loudly. This is the reason everyone on campus knows which child has AIDS or at least thinks they have AIDS. The truth is, these two kids really do have AIDS and cautionary measures should always be taken when dealing with them. It is still wrong for anyone to be putting their business out in the open the way Mr. Larry and other staff do…

Abraham (17 years old) and Corinthian (16 years old) are African-American teenagers who have been in the system almost all their lives. They both contracted AIDS from their mothers during birth. These children came in this world with a serious strike against them and their parents didn't do anything to make life better for them. Both parents are drug addicts whose only concern is when they will get their drug of choice again…

I certainly can understand why these kids are pissed off with life and don't give a damn about anyone else. They don't even care about themselves because they know that they are going to die from the AIDS virus someday. My heart really goes out to them. I will never think of them the way staff like Mr. Larry does. He is just ignorant and unsympathetic to be like that; he should be more considerate of what these children have to deal with knowing that they can't have anything that comes close to a normal life…

Mostly all the kids on campus are having unsafe sex, especially Abraham and Corinthian. Apparently these two kids don't mind sharing their virus with the other kids. Neither one seems concerned about spreading their death sentence to the other children. They both tell the other kids that they don't have AIDS and apparently the other kids believe them. I guess this is why they are able to still have sex in spite of the rumors that they have AIDS...

On several occasions Abraham has been caught having sex with some of the girls on campus. No one knows for sure why the girls on campus don't seem to believe that Abraham has AIDS, maybe they just have a death wish. Even if they just felt sorry for him I would think that they still would request that he use protection before they gave him any sex...

Corinthian creates even more of a problem because she dates boys and girls. She seems to change partners as often as she changes her clothes. Not too long ago she was dating an 18-year-old girl at St. Monica until the girl went home. There have been numerous occasions when Miss Janet caught Corinthian and her girlfriend in the bed together in the mornings when she came to work. Many staff sleep at night so is very easy for the girls to sneak into each other's rooms and spend the whole night together having sex. These uncaring staff makes it so easy for these kids to have sex anytime they want...

Corinthian has been questioned by staff on many occasions about having unprotected sex and her response is always the same. She rebelliously says, "I don't care if someone else gets a disease; didn't no one care when my mother gave me one, so forget them"...

If staff supervised properly, the kids wouldn't be able to have sex on the units so often; it always comes down to the staff doing their job. I also understand how hard it can be to do your job if you don't have enough staff working on the unit and that falls on the company. It is a vicious cycle that seems endless...

No one is for sure how many sex partners Corinthian and Abraham have had on this campus and other places that they have lived in the last five years. No one seems to be looking at the future outcome of all this sexual activity of these two individuals who have the AIDS virus. In the next 10 years, there could be thousands of AIDS cases that are the consequences of what happened on this campus with these two kids. There is simply no excuse for this behavior being allowed to happen on this campus or any campus. There will be a lot of needless deaths in the future because of the incompetence of this company and its leaders...

The parent of the girl that Corinthian was dating at St. Monica came to the main building upset and crying. She told the receptionist named Miss Lilly why she was so upset. The parent whose name is Miss Woods said, "One of the girls at St. Monica gave my baby AIDS and the staff let it happened by not supervising the kids. Now because of these lazy ass staff, my daughter has a death sentence because she got the AIDS virus from this girl named Corinthian. Why would this company have a child on campus that has AIDS anyway?" Miss Lilly firmly said, "You need to lower your voice and tell me who you want me to contact for you. You can save all that shit for someone who gives a damn". Miss Woods angrily said, "I want to talk to the supervisor of St. Monica right now". Miss Lilly calmly said, "Sit down and I will try to contact someone"...

Miss Lilly calls Mr. Derek over intercom as Miss Woods remains in the lobby verbally venting. Miss Woods was so noisy in the lobby that Miss Lilly had to close her door just to talk over the phone. She has been working at God's Love Institute for 20 years and has become quite accustomed to angry parents coming to the main lobby. Of course she is getting older now and getting pretty tired of putting up with the bullshit. She is anxiously looking forward to her retirement...

Miss Lilly quickly looks up as she hears loud noises in the lobby. Miss Woods is walking around the lobby kicking and knocking chairs over. She is pulling pictures off the walls and slamming them crashing to the floor. Angry words are coming out of her mouth, but Miss Lilly cannot understand what she is saying because the office door is closed. One thing for certain Miss Woods is definitely out of control. She considered calling the police, but decided that she would give Mr. Derek a few more minutes to get there. Even though her office door was closed and locked she can see very clearly through the glass window that showed the complete lobby...

Here's another case when campus security would be a great asset. However, hiring security guards would cut into God's Love Institute's profit and that's unthinkable for the company. Apparently money is more important than safety of staff and kids. God forbid that this company worries about the safety of their employees or the children...

Finally after 20 minutes of uncertainty for Miss Lilly, Mr. Derek arrives at the main lobby. He could see the mess that Miss Woods had made in the lobby so he approached her very cautiously. Mr. Derek is infamous for talking his way out of everything, especially work...

Before he could open his mouth, Miss Woods quickly rushed across the lobby and slapped the shit out of him. Her action took him totally by surprise and he had no defense for her. He is not a fighter; he is a talker and if he plans on winning this fight with Miss Woods then he is going to have to talk fast today...

His first impulse was to slap her back, but he opted to grab her arms so she couldn't slap him again. In spite of Miss Lilly's door being close, she could hear the slap across his face very clearly. It sounded like two large hands forcefully clapping together. She did everything in her power to keep herself from laughing out loud. In all her 20 years, she has never seen a parent attack a staff. She has always felt like someone should slap Mr. Derek and now she finally gets to see it. The slap across his face has made all her 20 years of putting up with bullshit worthwhile...

Miss Woods screams hysterically, "My daughter has AIDS because your people didn't do their job". Mr. Derek calmly said, "What are you talking about? Let's go to my office so we can have some privacy". He slowly let go of her arms, thinking she was ready to calm down. With one quick accurate move of a ninja, she kicked him in his privates sending him crashing to the floor in excruciating pain. He grabs his privates as pain permeates throughout his whole body. His mind is racing with confusion; he couldn't believe what was happening to him. He said, "You crazy bitch, what in the fuck is your damn problem? Have you lost your fucking mind?" Miss Woods said in a demonic voice, "I should kill you right now for what you let happened to my baby"...

Before Mr. Derek could respond, she quickly reached in her purse and pulled out what looked like a black snub-nosed 38 caliber pistol. With a crazed look on her face she pointed the deadly pistol directly at his head. Miss Lilly saw the gun and frantically grabbed the phone, then she wisely dove behind our desk. The movement that she made looked like something out of the movies except she did not have a stunt-double to take away the pain of diving on the hard floor. She wasn't worried about getting hurt; she just wanted to make sure she called the police before someone got shot...

With fear running through his body Mr. Derek Shouts, "Wait a minute we can work this out. You aren't going to be able to help your daughter if you're in prison for murder". Miss Woods said, "She's going to die so you should die also. Maybe I will kill all of the motherfuckers who work at the unit. They all deserve to die; I should have brought more bullets so I could kill everyone"...

Lying behind her desk Miss Lilly could hear every word that was being said in the lobby, but she dared not lift her head up to see what was going on. When this whole incident started it seemed like just another angry parent letting off steam, but now it has become a life or death situation. Miss Lilly knew that someone was going to get Mr. Derek someday for all the bullshit he has done in the past, but she really didn't expect this craziness...

Mr. Derek starts to cry as he looks down the barrel of the pistol. He is not only crying like a baby, tears are rapidly flowing from his eyes like a flooded river onto the floor. He is having thoughts of dying and never seeing his family again. He is having regrets about all the people that he had done wrong in the past and all the kids that he could've served better. He is wishing that he could go back and change his inconsiderate ways...

It is funny what pointing a pistol at a person would do to their mind. The crying apparently doesn't mean anything to Miss Woods because she continues to point the pistol directly at his head. She said, "Are you ready to go to hell for what you have done?" Suddenly just like in the movies the police came to the door with their guns drawn and pointing them at Miss Woods...

When Mr. Derek saw the police out the corner of his eye; he closed his eyes and began to loudly pray to God. He started begging God to spare his life. He desperately said, "Please give me another chance and I promise that I will make everything right". He thought for sure that she was going to quickly pull the trigger as soon as she saw the police...

Miss Woods said as he was praying, "If I would have known that you were such a bitch, I wouldn't have brought this gun with me. Looking at you down on the floor crying, I think I can beat your ass with my two little fists, you fucking faggot". The two policemen pointed their guns and shouted authoritatively through the glass door, "Dropped the fucking gun or we'll shoot! Drop it right now; this is your last warning"! She said with a half smile on her face, "The gun isn't real; it's a toy gun that I purchased at the dollar store on my way here". She dropped it on Mr. Derek's head and smiled as the hard plastic made a strange sound as it bounced off his head onto the floor. She said to Mr. Derek, "You're lucky motherfucker that all I wanted to do was scare you this time. If my daughter dies, then

I'm really going to kill you and your family". While he was lying on the floor breathing a sigh of relief, she balled her fist up tightly and punched him square in his mouth causing his bottom lip to bleed profusely...

She casually stepped over him and put her hands in the air as she walked out the door to surrender to the police. One of the policemen quickly ran inside the door and carefully picked up the pistol off the floor to examine it. After quickly checking the pistol he smiled and shouted back to the other officer, it's fake. He asked Mr. Derek was he okay and slowly helped him up off the floor. Mr. Derek did not respond to police officer's concerns; he was too busy wiping the blood and embarrassment off his face...

The police officer put Miss Woods in handcuffs and gently put her in the back seat of the police car. Both officers went back inside and asked Mr. Derek what he wanted them to do with Miss Woods. Mr. Derek angrily said, "I don't give a damn what you do with her, just get her off of this campus. Right now I want her arrested for assault and battery". The police officer said, "We are going to need someone to come to the station to sign the paperwork for these charges". Mr. Derek said, "I'll be there after I talk to my boss and see exactly where they want to go with this"...

After the police left, Miss Lilly came out of her office to see if she could help Mr. Derek. Even though she didn't like Mr. Derek, strangely a feeling of sorrow went through her body for him. She could sense that this man was humiliated and temporarily stripped of his manhood because of this incident...

Mr. Derek wasn't the only one praying when that gun was pointed towards his head. Miss Lilly started praying right after she got off the phone talking to the police about the gun. She prayed for both of their lives to be spared today and God came through for her as he always does. She has always said to other staff that it is going to take a lot of prayers to help Mr. Derek to change his ungodly ways...

She calmly said, "Mr. Derek will you be okay? Do you need a doctor?" He quietly said, "I'm fine, I was just putting on an act so she wouldn't shoot me". She smiled and said, "Boy that was a damn good act! If I had an Oscar, I would give you an "Academy award" for that performance". She smiled at him in a satisfying way and before he could respond, she calmly walked back into her office. Even after all that happened to him; he still can't stop himself from lying...

God's Love Institute decided not to press charges on Miss Woods because they wanted to keep the whole incident from getting too much publicity. The company certainly didn't want it in the news that they had children on the units sharing the AIDS virus with each other. Miss Lilly and Mr. Derek were admonished not to mention anything about the incident to anyone else on campus. The company really didn't have to tell Mr. Derek that because he was quite embarrassed about the whole situation anyway. That was a day in his life that he would gladly be quiet about. He didn't even tell his wife what happened that day...

However Miss Lilly didn't quite feel the same way; she started running her mouth five minutes after Mr. Derek walked out the door that day. She received a great deal of pleasure in telling everyone she knew about how Mr. Derek was on the floor crying like a baby. Within 24 hours everyone knew about Mr. Derek getting his ass beat at the main building. There was talk all over campus about him getting beat up by a 130 pound woman with a toy pistol, but there was no talk about trying to control the spread of the AIDS virus on campus. How ironic is that? The priorities on this campus are just completely fucked up...

Maybe this incident will be a wake-up call for Mr. Derek and this company. Maybe from now on we will see a new Mr. Derek, a more sympathetic one, a more understanding one. Maybe this situation will make him more humble. Maybe this is God's way of getting his attention and letting him know that it is

210

not about him and how he looks, it is about the children. Maybe he will be a start for all the positive changes that are needed on this campus. Maybe this is the way God intends to use him to make lives better for the children...

I know God has a plan even though sometimes I do not understand what it is. There have been many days when I asked God how he could let a person like Mr. Derek and some of the other staff work among troubled children. The answers to my prayers have not been made clear to me yet, but I have learned that the things in life that I cannot fix are to be handed off to God so that he can take care of him. We cannot fix all things in life, but we do have the ability to fix some things. For some time now, I have put God's Love Institute and the children who live there now and in the past; in God's worthy hands...

"Believe in Change"

Chapter 31

"Something strange happened"

*O*ne night Miss Donna was working at all-boys-unit. The ages of the boys are 8 to 15. There are 13 boys at this unit and most of the time there is only one staff available to work during the night shift. When this occurs, legally the company is out of compliance with DPW regulations. That's nothing new for this company because they are always short-staffed on the units. This company figures its okay since usually the boys are all sleeping at night and aren't going to cause any problems. It wouldn't matter if the boys were awake because the company doesn't have enough staff to cover to shift anyway...

Some female staff are uncomfortable working at an all boys unit alone. This is understandable because there is nothing to stop these boys if they wanted to beat the staff up or even rape the female staff. The female staff certainly can't defend themselves against 13 boys if that was to happen. These kids have many issues that need to be addressed by a professional and not the staff that they hire on the units. That isn't who God's Love Institute hires because that would mean they would have to pay more money...

About an hour into Miss Donna's Shift, a 13-year-old named Roman quietly came to his door to ask to go use the bathroom. All the boys on the unit know that they aren't supposed to come to their door unless they have more than just their underwear on. They are even supposed to have their upper body covered at all times outside of their room. All the kids know the rules, but some of the kids have to find out which staff takes these rules seriously. Some staff simply don't give a damn what the boys have on when they leave their rooms. This is just another way of keeping the poor kids confused. The rules are simple, but they just have to be enforced consistently to work properly. Slowly sticking his head out the door, Roman anxiously said "Miss I need to go to the bathroom?" She softly said, "Okay and don't be all day". She assumed that he knew to have the appropriate clothing on so she didn't even mention it to him. This is her first time working at this unit and she had never heard anything bad about the boys at this unit...

Miss Donna is a cute white female in her early 20s. She has long dark brown hair that rides down her back. She is only 5 feet tall, weighing about 120 pounds which created a very sexy figure for the boys and the staff on campus to admire...

In order to get to the bathroom Roman has to walk pass Miss Donna, who is sitting in the hallway watching TV. She is so busy watching TV that she didn't pay any attention to Roman walking down the hall until he said, "Hi Miss what's on TV?" When Miss Donna slowly looked his way she saw a hard penis staring at her. Her face began instantly red with embarrassment and shock...

For whatever reason, when Roman got directly in front of Miss Donna his penis popped straight out of his boxer underwear. Only he knows if his penis was hard before he left his room or if it is suddenly gets hard as he was walking down a hallway. Miss Donna wasn't paying any attention when he left his room so she doesn't know if it was hard before he left the room. She angrily said, "Put that damn thing away, I don't want to see that. Go back to your room until you can figure out what to do with that thing and don't come out until you have some pants on". He proudly smiles and walked slowly back to his room. She loudly said, "When you figure it out, then you can come and use the bathroom"...

Two minutes later, Roman quickly comes to his door and says, "Miss I can't get it in my pants and I'm not sure what to do". Now she's beginning to think that Roman is simply messing with her because he can't be that dumb. Irritated she said, "You aren't going to use the bathroom until you figure out how to put it away, I don't care if you fucking piss on yourself"...

Five minutes later with tears beginning to form in his eyes Roman says, "I got to go to the bathroom real bad, do you have any suggestions for me". She thought to herself, "If he wants to mess with me then I'm going to fix his retarded ass". She found some duct tape and rolled it down the hallway towards his room. She smiled and said, "There's some duct tape in the hall, use that to tape it down". Roman quickly runs out in the hall and grabs the tape. After struggling to tape his penis down for five minutes, he thinks that he's ready to come out his room. He has his penis taped tightly to his leg causing him to walk like he has a wooden leg. He proudly said, "I did what you told me to do, but I can't get my pants on and I really have to use the bathroom". She reluctantly said, "Okay but I better not see your damn penis again"...

He cautiously limped pass Miss Donna and when he got to the bathroom he realized he had to unloosened the duct tape to take a piss. By this time he felt like he was ready to bust from holding his piss for so long. After desperately struggling with the tape, he took a two minute piss. He meticulously put the tape back on his still hard penis. Slowly he walked towards Miss Donna hoping the tape with continued to hold his now painful penis to his leg...

She is curious about how he used the tape, but fought the urge to ask him. Roman could feel the tape weakening with each step towards his room. He is having visions of his penis popping out and poking Miss Donna in the eye. He stops suddenly and stands motionless a few feet away from where Miss Donna is sitting. She nervously said, "Why are you standing there? You need to get to your room, it's getting late". With fear in his voice he said, "I think the tape is going to come loose and I don't want you to get mad at me. I'm not sure what to do". Now she is starting to feel like he is really messing with her and she is getting tired of it. She said, "Here is stapler to use for stapling your underwear close so it won't pop out again". She threw it to him and watched as he struggled to staple the opening of his boxer underwear...

Miss Donna focused her attention back on the TV until suddenly she heard a painful scream come from Roman. She quickly looked up and saw Roman rolling around on the floor holding his groin area. The look on his face indicated that he was in excruciating pain. She knew by that look that he wasn't playing around. Miss Donna said, "What's wrong Roman and why are you hollering like that". He said as his voice was breaking up, "I think that I stapled my penis by mistake". She said, "Go to your room and try to pull the staple out". He struggled to his feet and ran to his room...

She sat and waited, hoping that he could get the staple out without taking him to the hospital; she definitely didn't want that kind of attention. After several attempts Roman said, "I got the staple out Miss, what do you want me to do with it". She said, "Throw it away because I don't want it. Is your penis feeling better now?" Roman said in a high pitched voice, "It hurts like hell and is bleeding a little. It's not hard anymore; I think the staple let the air out of it. Now it is deflated like a busted balloon". She smiled and said, "You need to go to sleep before you get into some more trouble". She was hoping that she could avoid writing an Incident Report on what happened tonight. Miss Donna wasn't sure how she could explain what happened in writing or even talking about it. She didn't expect all of this to happen tonight. She had to admit to herself that things did get a little out of control. Sometimes she forgets what kind of kids she is working with...

It is surprisingly quiet the rest of the night except for an occasional painful moan and groan coming from Roman's room. Miss Donna is happily gone by the time Roman wakes up in the morning. She consciously decided not to mention the incident to the morning staff. Hopefully Roman doesn't mention it and the whole incident will fade away like never happen just like most incidents on this campus...

When the morning staff woke up Roman, he complained briefly about his penis hurting. The staff didn't pay any attention to his complaints because they are accustomed to hearing the kids complain in the morning. They figured he was up all night masturbating like most of the kids do in Residential living...

Roman continued to get dressed for school in spite of a constant throbbing pain coming from his penis. Roman goes to school on campus so he doesn't have to walk very far to get to class. He has a peculiar limp when he walks, but the staff really doesn't care. They are just happy to get the kids to school without a restraint so they can go back to the units and go to sleep. Once the kids arrive at the school, the staff who works for education are in charge of them until they go back over to the units in the afternoon...

There is minimal communication between the education staff and the unit staff. Most of the staff at the school is schoolteachers except for the big muscle-bound or fat guys who sit in the hallway and do the restraints on the kids for the teachers. Over the years the two groups have found very little to agree about when it comes to the treatment of the kids. The teachers are never on the units so they have never experienced what the staff on the units has to deal with when interacting with the kids. If the teachers never experience what it's like to work on the units than they will never understand the how the unit staff feel. Needless to say, there will always be conflict and animosity between the teachers and the staff from the units...

Roman's math teacher named Miss Porter noticed the obvious pain in his every movement and asked him what is wrong. She said, "Roman why are you walking like you have been riding a horse too long?" He said, "You really don't want to know Miss, trust me when I say that". She confidently said, "I have been teaching for a long time, there is nothing that I haven't heard before". He boldly said, "Okay, but I told you that you didn't want to know. I accidentally stapled my penis last night at the unit and it hurts like hell". The other kids, both boys and girls begin laughing hysterically and making fun of Roman...

The class got so out of control that the teacher had to ask the hall monitors to help her regain control of the class. The teacher pulled Roman to the side and asked if he was serious. He said, "Yes Miss, it happened on the unit with Miss Donna". The teacher said, "Do you want to see the nurse?" He said, I think I better because my penis doesn't look right"...

The hall monitors escorted him over to the nurse's office, which is located in the Main Building on the second floor. The nurse was shocked and devastated to find out how Roman's penis got injured. He had bruises and abrasions all over his penis. However she didn't believe him because the story was too crazy to be true. She knew that these kids can be very creative, but she has never heard a story quite like this. She wrote the information down, but she decided to do some investigation before she reported the incident to anyone. She figured that this was another case of extreme masturbation by one of the kids...

A few days later the nurse questioned Miss Donna and she told her the same wild story that Roman did. Except for the fact that Roman's story was a little more colorful than Miss Donna's version. The nurse told Miss Donna that some people may not be too happy with how she handled that situation. Miss Donna rebelliously said, "I don't care, what are they going to do fire me or something"...

A week later after Mr. Derek talked to Roman and Miss Donna; something very strange happened during the conversation with Miss Donna. To everyone's recollection what happened is a history breaking event on this campus. Here is some idea as to how rare and strange it is. There have been more people struck by lightning in the last 100 years then what happened to Miss Donna. It's so unbelievable that it took Miss Donna three days to fathom what happened to her...

When the word of what happened to her got out, it spread across campus like the winds of a tornado. Now Miss Donna is infamous in the eyes of all the unit staff who works at God's Love Institute because of what the company did to her that day. I know reading this makes you wonder what I'm talking about that is so unusual. Well I didn't believe it at first either until Miss Donna actually showed me the paperwork. There were some words on the paperwork that was never mentioned or written before by any supervisor that I know of on this campus...

Miss Donna had trouble telling people and I'm having trouble reading it. This is what happened that was so strange, Mr. Derek wrote Miss Donna up for "Unprofessional Conduct" because of the incident with the Roman. No one has ever been written up for unprofessional conduct before. No one can recall a time when this company actually used that terminology ever. God's Love Institute has learned some new words and I wonder if they are ever going to use them again. What's next is the company going to start making the staff actually do their job now? **"Believe in Change"**

Final Chapter 32

"Reflections"

*R*eflecting back over the years that I've worked with these troubled youth in Residential Living, I am still finding it hard to find anything substantially positive to say about my experience. I certainly wish that I could have done more to help these children, but the way these institutions are run makes that almost impossible for now...

I do have some good news to share with the readers of this book. Sister Lucy has step down or has been fired from her position. Thank God for that because she hasn't done anything for the children that I know of in the last three years. She has been with this company for 30 years and she is the main reason, in my opinion that God's Love Institute has become a living hell for these poor mislead children...

For a long time she knew what was going on in residential living and turned her back to it. She stood back and watched as child abuse cases, one after another got swept under the rugs of betrayal. For the years that I've seen her, the only thing she did is organize fundraisers "It's all about the money". It appears to me that for many years she has forgotten what this organization is supposed to stand for. If the leader of this company doesn't give a damn, why should the people below her care. Her job has now been taken over by Sister Rosa; I am not sure how long she has been with this company. I don't believe she can do any worse than Sister Lucy. The title of Sister should stand for something other than just a "CEO" and how much money can a company make. The term "Nun" is synonymous with the work of God. Let's do the work like you are "Sisters of Christ"!!!

Mr. Derek and Miss Lisa were demoted from their positions of power. Mr. Derek was demoted because he never did a damn thing that looked like work. Miss Lisa was demoted because she watched him not do a damn thing. Now they will have more time to continue their alleged campus romance. Their affair was the only thing that they were good at anyway because they didn't do a damn thing positive for kids or the staff. They certainly made a lot of money from this company by stealing from the kids. The two of them should be fired instead of demoted. Hopefully their demotion is the beginning of their end. If either Miss Lisa or Mr. Derek has the pleasure of reading this book, do everyone a favor and never worked with kids again. You both are a disgrace to this career field so please look deep into your hearts and souls and find something else to do with your lives. The world will be a lot better off, especially for the helpless kids in residential living...

This year is supposedly a transitional year for God's Love Institute in many positive ways. The demotion of Sister Lucy, Mr. Derek and Miss Lisa is only supposed to be the beginning of a better living for the children in residential living...

The head of the Education Department named Dr. Dickson was fired for misuse of funds. He was another person that never did shit and the company finally did something about it. These kids didn't learn anything in God's Love Institute at the campus school, but the company got paid a lot of money for having the useless program...

The rumor is that this company is losing money now or not making as many millions as they use to. I can believe that especially considering they pay over $1 million in overtime each and every year that I have been here. They have just recently cut back the staff's overtime hours to only 60 hours a pay period. For the last three years most of the staff has gotten used to having over a hundred hours in overtime. Most of the staff that works here makes $9-$10 an hour, but with overtime they make over $40,000 a year without a college degree or doing any real work with the children...

I remember the first time I met Mr. Moe (One of the infamous Three Stooges) and he said proudly, "Where else can you work and make $40,000 a year for watching TV and playing video games". He was right, except he left out two other things and that is he also got to abuse children and steal from them whenever he wanted to. If you decide to purchase this book Mr. Moe, I just want to let you know that I did report you for stealing the shoulder pads from one of the boy's units. Mr. Derek just didn't do anything about it as usual. You are the worst kind of thief; you steal from poor children...

Where are the success stories for all the kids that God's Love Institute supposedly helped? How many kids go off to college? How many kids become doctors and lawyers? The truth is more kids end up in prison than go to college. After being in business for a hundred years, I would think that this company would have many success stories to brag about. The truth is, I have not heard of one yet and I have been here for years...

Just in the last two weeks I have read negative stories about two 15 year old kids that used to be here. One was killed in a gang related shooting and the other was arrested for killing an innocent 12-year-old girl in a drive-by shooting. Since I have been working at God's Love Institute, this has been the typical outcome for these children. I doubt if God's Love Institute will even acknowledge that these two boys resided here. No one at this company seems to care once they stop receiving a paycheck for these kids. There has to be more done to save these kids lives because it is life or death once they leave this company. The only thing that I have seen God's Love Institute be successful at is making millions of dollars and now they aren't good at that anymore...

This company needs to put something in place to measure how effective their treatments for these kids are. These

221

statistics should start from admission to departure. The vast percentages of the children who come here suffer from school problems, aggression, being out of parental control, and depression. That is just to name a few of the problems these children have. When these children come to a residential program, it should be a safe, structured family environment. This is necessary just to address their basic needs that are constantly being taken for granted. The child's basic needs will be the foundation for positive growth. Most of these children have broken or fractured spirits that are never going to be repaired if they are never addressed during their transition into Residential living. God is going to have to be slowly, but consistently mixed into these children's lives if we are ever going to hear about a success story...

If you have read this book then you will know that none of this is in place at God's Love Institute. There are children who have been diagnosed with mental health disorders and need to receive counseling and treatment through a behavior health service program. I have talked to the psychologist who work on campus and all of them are dissatisfied with the way God's Love Institute runs things. Their biggest complaint is that the company will not let them do their jobs and their job is to help make the child better. I personally know of one therapist who had to take time off because she was on the verge of a nervous break-down because of the stress the company have put on her by not supporting how she needs to do her job...

What the children get at God's Love Institute is the Three Stooges (Curly, Moe and Larry) who know nothing about mental health. However they are allowed to work at Residential Therapeutic Facility (RTF) unit for years and no one gives a damn. At a (RTF) unit, this company can make up to $600 per child for a single day. Instead of paying a college graduate with a degree in psychology, an appropriate amount of money to work here, the company would rather pay the Three Stooges $9-$10 an hour. It's all about the money!!!

There is a rumor in the air that God's Love Institute is going to change the way they do things completely. They are going to change over into a "Kids Town" organization; that has been in business for 90 years. They boast that they have 90 years of saving children and families. Kids Town provides residential, education, and hospital care for more than 47,000 homeless, abuse, neglected, and handicapped youth. This company does all this regardless of race or creed...

They also assisted nearly 450,000 children and families through their "Kids Town National Hot Line", and indirectly reached almost a million more. I wonder how much of this is really true or is this just something they say or write when they're requesting contributions. I am sure that God's Love Institute has similar literature that they send out when they're requesting donations. I have yet to hear of a place that actually does what it says. I have committed a lot of my prayers to finding an organization that is truly concerned with helping children. Maybe Kids Town is God's answer to my prayers. Time will tell...

I would like to thank all the employees at God's Love Institute who in spite of what the company said, decided to purchase a copy of my book. Almost all of the employees that I've met in my years at God's Love Institute have told me that they are unhappy with the company. This unhappiness that you have expressed to me should not go unresolved because life is too short to live like that. The employees are going to have to be more proactive in their happiness. This unhappiness is contagious and will permeate down to the helpless children who are in residential living...

Either do something about your unhappiness or stop working with children. Stop making life more difficult than what it is. Working with children starts from the heart and transmits through the actions of your life. Anyone that knows anything about this business of working with children knows that you are not going to make a lot of money doing this. Stop moaning and groaning and do something to find your happiness because happiness is not just going to come to you. The staff may not know this, but damn near everyone you know is tiring of hearing you bitch about God's Love Institute. There are other jobs, other cities that you can find your happiness so don't just settled for something that makes you unhappy...

When I came to work at God's Love Institute, I did not go there to make money. I wanted to help children; if I wanted to make money I would have gone somewhere else. These children need your help more than ever and if you're not able to give 100% then you shouldn't work with children...

It takes a special person to decide to work with troubled youth and not be concerned with how much money they are going to make. I have not met a special person like that at God's Love Institute. There are some decent people who work there, but they should not be working with children. They do not have that gift, but I'm sure they have a talent that is definitely being wasted working with children. The staff just has to find out what their talent is and they can't do that if they continue to do something that makes them unhappy...

I believe if something makes you unhappy (especially work) then it's probably not the work you should be doing. I cannot tell the staff what to do, but I believe I'm qualified to tell them what not to do. This is what I say to some of the staff that I have met at God's Love Institute, "Do not work with kids if you are more concerned with making money because you can not make money working with kids in residential living"...

A bus driver in Hopesville can make $49,000-$90,000 a year. A garbage man can make $50,000-$70,000 a year. A school janitor can make $50,000 a year. These three jobs only require a high school diploma. There are staff that have master's degrees at God's Love Institute and have to beg to get $40,000 a year. Our children are supposed to be this country's greatest asset yet they will spend more money to have trash picked up. Where is the incentive to get an education if you can get $90,000 a year to drive a bus with a high school diploma? Our society constantly sends mixed signals to our children. No wonder confusion runs rampant among our young people...

There is power in numbers and if all the Educators in United States come together as a whole; we can probably make a difference and more money. I believe that there are too many egos in education and not enough strong leaders. We are going to need strong leaders to change the way these children are being treated, especially in residential living. Everyone that works in this career field believes they have an answer to the problems that the children of today are having. All these answers will not mean a thing until we find strong leaders to compliment the answers. Let's focus more on leadership instead of the answers to the problems of the children at risk. I have invited other educators to give their input on what direction they believe would best help the children of today. As you can see, none of them thought it was important enough to share their insight in this book...

I hope you enjoyed reading this book because Mr. Renaldo sure did not enjoy working at God's Love Institute. I wrote this book because I wanted people to know what really goes on at this organization and I believe many others across the United States. This organization is no different than any other one that does this kind of work. You can go anywhere in the United States and hear stories about children being abused at these organizations...

The stories in this book come from what Mr. Renaldo seen and what he heard from the kids and other staff. I don't know if me putting these stories in writing are going to make a difference for these children. If this book helps one child have a better experience with any of these companies then it was worth writing for me...

When my editor read this book he thought that I titled the book wrong because I said that the book is based on true stories. He simply couldn't believe that all of these stories in this book are based on true stories. It took some convincing, but now he has come around and you will also if you look a little deeper into Residential living in the United States...

Once this book is released there will be many people who will come to me and ask me if these stories are true. If you don't believe me or the stories that I have written, then just ask anyone who works with children in residential living. I can almost guarantee that you might hear even worse stories than the ones I have written in this book...

I actually have more stories, but I didn't want to overwhelm you by putting them all in one book. I have enough stories to write 10 books. If you want to hear more stories or read more stories either talk to me or keep your eyes open for the next copy of **"Children on Layaway; Its all about the Money$$$"**... **"Believe in Change"**

The End...

About the Author

Ron Howard, (The Author) is a graduate of the University of Pittsburgh with degrees in **"Applied Developmental Psychology"** and **"Child and Family Studies")** and he is currently pursuing a Masters Degree, **"Specializing in Program Design and Leadership"** also at the University of Pittsburgh. He has a **"Black Belt in Shotokan Karate"** from the Uniontown Karate School in Uniontown PA... He is a "Primary Youth Counselor" working with troubled youth ages (6 to 18). He has **"Daycare Director Credentials"** for the state of Pennsylvania. He is currently writing his third book titled **"First Blood, the summer of Power"**; at your request, there will be a sequel to my first book **"From the bottom to the Top, the Jackson Street Dreamer"**. Let me hear from you at jacksonstreetdreamer@yahoo.com "God Bless" and keep reading...

Thank You for reading my book.... **"Believe in Change"**

Ron Howard Writer/Author